LEAD FOLLOW OR GET OUT OF THE WAY

Lessons Learnt in THE SPECIAL FORCES

ABHAY NARAYAN SAPRU

First published 2026
Reprinted 2026

ISBN 978-81-8328-695-4 (PB)
ISBN 978-81-8328-702-9 (HB)

Published by
Wisdom Tree
4779/23, Ansari Road
Darya Ganj, New Delhi-110 002
Ph.: 011-23247966/67/68
wisdomtreebooks@gmail.com

Printed in India

Beginning with its title, this book is filled with powerful leadership lessons. The battlefield anecdotes are invaluable, offering rare insight into decision-making under pressure. Abhay's blend of frontline military experience and senior corporate leadership uniquely positions him to draw sharp, meaningful parallels. Whether you are already a senior leader or aspiring to become one, this book is a true gem—and an absolute must-read.

—Manish Shah, MD & CEO, Godrej Capital

This book is unique—a master class combining the author's experience while serving with the Special Forces and the corporate world, as well as his knowledge and individual pursuits outside these spheres. The interrelation between the brain and brawn and training one's mind has been beautifully enumerated, interspersed with operational anecdotes that are educative and blunt. The takeaways are excellent, collectively summarising not only what leadership is all about, but also how life should be lived. After his three excellent novels based on live operations, this is a superlative fourth, which should be read by everyone.

—Lt Gen PC Katoch, PVSM, UYSM, AVSM, SC (Retd), Parachute Regiment (SF)

This book, *Lead, Follow or Get Out of the Way*, by Abhay Narayan Sapru, brings together real-world experiences and meaningful lessons that speak directly to today's professionals. His reflections show how character, judgement and resilience shape outcomes in challenging moments. Young managers will find in its pages a valuable compass for navigating an increasingly complex world. It is a compelling read for anyone serious about leadership that endures beyond circumstance.

—Dr HK Pradhan, Prof of Finance and Economics, XLRI Jamshedpur

This book is just the truth of a man who has lived what he writes. And that truth stays with you.

—Vidhu Vinod Chopra, Filmmaker

The intense lessons of the battlefield—which can take years to learn in 'real life'—are distilled and delivered in this remarkable book. Major Sapru has done an extraordinary job of drawing parallels and integrating corporate strategy with military leadership. Highly recommended for management professionals and students; this is an essential read.

—Saibal Ghosh, Chief Investment Officer,
Bandhan Life Insurance

Major Abhay Narayan Sapru distils battlefield wisdom into practical lessons on courage and decisive action. This is a crisp, engaging book that helps the reader to hone their leadership skills as it brings clarity to everyday leadership thoughts. Excellent book as it is not only inspiring, but also useful for anyone seeking to lead with purpose under challenging situations.

—Dr Debashis Sanyal, Director, Great Lakes
Institute of Management, Chennai

Drawing from his rare experience in both the Special Forces and senior leadership roles in Indian banking, Abhay Sapru distils powerful lessons on leadership, discipline, teamwork and decision-making. *Lead, Follow, or Get Out of the Way* is a compelling narrative that demonstrates how principles forged in the most demanding environments of the armed forces are deeply relevant to leadership in industry—and to life itself.

—Dr Ajit Parulekar, Director, Goa Institute of Management

This book, like all the other earlier ones, is dedicated to my parents. Wish you could have been around to read them, and to Colonel Sahib, a big thanks for introducing me to the profession of Arms.

To the Special Forces and especially the First Battalion: Thanks. Some of the experiences and learnings cannot be rendered in words. One must go through the process; pity the uninitiated will never know of this.

Finally, to Ritu, Shraddha and Ary for shaking me out of my languor.

CONTENTS

WHY I WROTE THIS BOOK AND WHY YOU SHOULD READ IT

This book, I guess, was never meant to be. However, like a lot of unplanned events in life, my putting pen to paper for this one, so to say, came about in an accidental manner. I served in the Special Forces (SF) for a decade, and for many years thereafter, it was a string of companies and MNC banks that employed me. During this time, I went through the usual grind and discomfort of first understanding the average civilian mindset and thereafter negotiating my way up the corporate ladder. Two decades later, I retired from the corporate world as a senior group president from a private bank. The journey from camouflage to corporate was, in hindsight, smoother than expected. Perhaps it was because of my hard training in the SF, my way of thinking and my attitude, all forged in very trying conditions.

I was not especially rich, but the return on effort was certainly satisfying. To me, wealth has always been relative to one's needs. Anything less can be stressful and anything more is often superfluous. By the end, autonomy held more value for me than wealth. All that was needed was more vigorous work, a desire for larger responsibility and a simmering fire in the belly to grow. But my course was run, or I understood myself, better with age.

The above qualities fundamentally conflicted with my temperament, which follows too seriously what Chekhov said, 'When a man spends the least possible movement over some definite action, that is grace.' Give me ease and comfort any day over toil and labour. However, compared to my time in the SF, the two decades stint out of the uniform was easy. Clearly, it struck me, certain tangible and intangible factors must have aided my growth, making the journey a pleasant experience. Sticking to the intangibles—the training, qualities and values imbibed while I was in the army and the SF, made this transition and progress a lot easier.

While I served in the army, and certainly for a decade thereafter, the nation had not awakened to the nationalistic fervour it is experiencing now. Generations of officers and men from my time and before me quietly went about their business of protecting the nation without ever talking or writing about their experiences. In any case, nobody outside the services was either listening or interested. The 1971 war was an event of the past and the various regional insurgencies were relegated to the periphery of national consciousness and ring-fenced physically by the army to contain a spill over into the hinterland. 'What the eye does not see, the mind does not know.'

Then the Kargil War happened.

The army was back in the spotlight and the media had a huge hand to play in it. In the years that followed, a couple of retaliatory trans-border raids, both on the eastern and western fronts, thrust the SF into public consciousness. The Bollywood movie *Uri* further etched the mystique of the SF, and the nation, enamoured by their exploits, suddenly had a new hero on the block. As they said about Clint Eastwood, 'Every boy dreamt of becoming and every man regretted he never was.' Deep down, every young man dreams of pitching himself against fearful odds and regrets he never really got around to testing himself. The SF, in a way, provided that chance for self-exploration.

Once I reached senior management, the HR departments in some of the corporates I worked for and a few outside asked me to give talks on the usual subjects of leadership and motivation. Having attended a few such workshops personally, I realised the huge anomaly that existed between teaching and practising, especially regarding some of the lessons dished out mostly by the so-called gurus on the subject, many of whom frankly had never truly put into practice what they were teaching.

One of the problems I faced when deciding the content of my talks was the difference in quality between the men I had served with in the SF and the intended audience, which mostly consisted of the junior and middle management in the company. To treat them at par would not only be naïve on my part but also a gross waste of time for both parties. They were not volunteers, had not been put through a rigorous selection process, were certainly not trained as a body of men and most importantly, would never face situations demanding extreme physical discomfort, life-threatening violence, split-second decisions and the enormous ramifications of failure, at times with national implications.

In due course of time, I was invited for a few podcasts, which I reluctantly accepted primarily to please my publisher, whose constant refrain was about my complete disinterest in promoting my books. I was pleasantly surprised by the response; many of the youngsters who had heard me or read my books got back with all sorts of questions in their feedback, mostly seeking guidance and advice on how to achieve goals and lead fulfilling, wholesome lives. It dawned on me that the younger generation was plagued by utter confusion, lack of direction and a flailing will. They had dreams and aspirations, but lacked the will and the consistency of labour necessary to achieve them. As my son once remarked quoting a famous author, 'The youth today, dad, is wasted on the young.' This book is for them.

Let me first simplify the mystique of the SF in the Indian context. In an approximately 1.3-million-strong volunteer army, which already has its own basic selection process, one has to re-volunteer for a probation to the SF. Anyone under the age of 26 from any arm of the army can volunteer. A 90-day probation, which tests the candidate physically, mentally and psychologically is carried out. The SF believe firmly in the adage, 'It is not possible to know how much is just enough unless one has experienced how much is more than enough.'

Following this dictum to the letter, they push you to your extremes to discover the chink in your armour and gauge your limits. Rejection rates are high and the handful of those selected is then rigorously trained till all necessary skills and actions become muscle memory. In fact, they discourage competitive sports since it diverts focus from the job at hand, preferring instead that individuals devote the same time to training. The system is further designed to allow any candidate to de-volunteer at any stage during his tenure for a myriad of reasons or to be RTU (returned to his parent unit) at the behest of the commanding officer, who had the authority to do so.

Despite forming under 1 per cent of the army's strength, battalions of the Parachute regiment (all converted to SF now) have earned 8 Ashok Chakras, 14 Maha Vir Chakras, 22 Kirti Chakras, 63 Vir Chakras, 32 Chief of Army Staff (COAS) citations and hundreds of other minor decorations for gallantry since independence. Over the years, the SF units have regularly won the Army Chief's Unit Citation, a prestigious honour awarded to the best unit in recognition of exemplary performance. This has all come about at the cost of the highest loss of life to both officers and other ranks, as compared to the rest of the line regiments of the army, especially during the many so-called low-intensity conflicts in the subcontinent.

So, at any given time, you have a body of volunteers trained to perfection, in peak physical shape and highly motivated. They are there because they want to be and for no other reason whatsoever. This bunch of men need no motivational or leadership talks. I recall being part of only two such talks in my entire time with them and I mention them in the book later. A poster in the adjutant's office in my unit comes to mind, which said, 'People join us not because we are different. But because they are.' Another one summed up very succinctly the ethos of the trade. It had a picture of a sheep pen with a sheep dog standing in attendance around the flock and it said, 'In here we either follow, lead or get out of the way.' You were trained to follow or lead as the occasion demanded and if neither, to make sure you were not a hindrance in the process. I thought it made a pertinent title for the book.

If I may add here, since I am often asked who is better amongst the various special units in India, i.e., the National Security Guard (NSG), Marine Commandos (MARCOS), Garuda Commando Force (Air Force) or the Parachute SF. Furthermore, comparisons are often drawn with the British SAS or the now-famous US Navy SEALs. Briefly, as far as the Indian context is concerned, the difference lies in the tasking. Building-intervention or anti-hijack operations are handled by the NSG; special operations on the high seas and maritime warfare are addressed by the MARCOS; the Garuda is for airfield protection and similar terrorist operations in connection with airfields; and the Para SF units are for external operations such as raids, ambushes, reconnaissance or any other operation in conjunction with the main conventional forces. Over time, they have been extensively used internally in all the insurgencies arising within the country.

The comparison with the foreign SF is specious, as it is the country's geopolitical ambitions, external threats and economic strengths that dictate the quality and quantity of its SF. These premises determine the selection criteria, strength, training and equipping of the force. The SF in the country now is vastly different from the one I served in, which was deplorably equipped; the elitism, as we jokingly used to say amongst ourselves, was more a product of the mind and the training rather than the possession of any sort of special military hardware.

So, the question was: what such qualities could be shared with my corporate colleagues that would be relevant to them in their professional and personal lives? The only thing I was sure of was the exclusion of leadership and motivation from my talk. This was purely because it is an oft-repeated topic in any company that consumes the bulk of the HR training budget, along with my awareness of my own inadequacies on the subject. I did not feel qualified enough to lecture anybody on the topics. But I do know a bit about character. That is what this book explores—not in formulae, but in anecdotes, reflections and a few borrowed incidents. However, both motivation and leadership are covered, as I see them, in independent chapters in the book.

Temperamentally, I tend to procrastinate, show mental indolence and have a fertile imagination often veering towards negativity. These are huge impediments to any kind of growth in life, as you will agree. But from time to time, I can shake off the lethargy and commit myself to positive action. It is because of these brief phases of heightened activity that I have managed to achieve some semblance of progress. This book is clearly a product of one of those constructive phases. Another aspect was to ensure that I stemmed any backward movement in life. As the saying goes in American prisons, 'In here, if you take one step back, you will never take another step forward.'

Clearly, one of the biggest achievements for me was to have made it into the SF. I took one look at the men around me and realised early on that if I could be 50 per cent of what these men were, my life would be enriched and the uncertainties and pitfalls on the journey of life negotiated with comparative ease. Amongst my contemporaries in the group, Jag Kairon clearly set the tone of life to be followed once we were out of uniform. Master, as he is fondly called, led the field in pushing the envelope, be it long runs, starting a business or embracing life with pure *joie de vivre.* Most of us saw the benefits and quietly followed in his wake. My mother was correct when she recommended that I keep the fellowship of positive, inquiring and happy people. The benefits are enormous.

So, if you are motivated, diligent and ambitious with a clear path to your goals, the book will give you ideas to improve and perhaps motivate you further to push your limits. But if you have limitations in these areas or lack these qualities for the most part while still harbouring dreams of leading an accomplished life, this book could prove even more beneficial.

This book is not a guide to promotions or peak performance. It is about balance—growth that is both vertical (professional stature) and horizontal (mental clarity, intellectual depth and the joy of hobbies). While many of these reflections stem from my time in the SF, they are not exclusive to that world. Most lessons here are intertwined and can resonate across personal and professional spheres.

You would not find exercises or flowcharts inside. Think of this more as a collection of essays—personal reflections, really. As Marco Polo once said, 'Things seen as seen and things heard as heard—I wrote it all down.' Some thoughts are tucked into chapters rather than standing alone, with end-of-chapter summaries to bring them together.

To be clear, this is not a manual on how military discipline can optimise your quarterly metrics. It does not promise Six Sigma or sharpened KPIs. It is simply an honest account of experiences—on the front lines and off them. Take what serves you.

THE DESK IS A DANGEROUS PLACE FROM WHICH TO VIEW THE WORLD

Faire et se taire (*Shut up and Get on with It*).

–Gustave Flaubert

It is early morning, and the shadows in the forest have yet to lift off. An SF patrol somewhere in Mannar, Sri Lanka, winds its way cautiously through the waist-high scrub heading towards the forest. Right behind the two scouts, I briefly pause and scan the forest in the near distance. A low mist still hangs over the canopy and its dark recesses conjure up images in my mind of the violence it could unleash. It looks malevolent. I am a rookie field captain having just cleared my probation. The temporary captain rank on my shoulder sits heavy and is there only because three senior captains are dead and another five wounded and out of action. Sri Lanka is the army's hard school, where you learn fast on the job or perish. Desultory thoughts cross my mind as I tell the scouts to swing left and head for the forest line.

I hear the radio operator behind me take a call and as I turn, he hands over the handset to me. 'Two-One,' he says. That is my boss, the team commander, who is sitting at a Gurkha battalion post and monitoring the couple of patrols that are out in the field.

'Two-One for Two-Two, pass over,' I say, and then all hell breaks loose on the net from the other end. There is alarm and panic in the major's voice, and for the first time, I hear him use expletives. If the tenor is enough to get my attention, the words pouring out in a high-pitched staccato turn my blood to ice.

'You have walked into an ambush, Two-Two. He is going to open fire at any moment. Spread out,' so on and so forth. The major is still spewing instructions as I drop the handset and glance towards the forest. I know he is sitting somewhere at the edge, watching. I can feel his presence. For many seconds, which seem an eternity, I stand rooted to the spot, unsure what to do next, waiting for the bullets to hit me. A myriad of conflicting thoughts goes through my mind. The foremost is of my mother, who will surely follow me if my innings ends here. My expression must have betrayed my emotions, since I see the men behind me gently go down to a kneeling position. I sensibly follow suit. We stay in that position for the next hour before I make my next move.

Apparently, a conversation between the Liberation Tigers of Tamil Eelam (LTTE; Tamil Tigers or Tigers in short) ambush leader and his commander in camp was intercepted by the divisional signals unit, who quickly pinpointed the general location and track the team commander at the post. The Tiger leader is taking permission to engage. He mentions the patrol strength and the SF unit we belong to from the distinctive black headgear (bandana) we wear. On being queried by the commander, he states that he could drop a couple, including the officer, but the rest were well spaced out and could manoeuvre around his position, as he was close and did not have enough guns. He is fortunately ordered to break contact, cease all movement and fall back to a certain point in the jungle. If we are foolish enough to cross that line, he is to decimate the patrol to the last man.

It was meant to be a 36-hour operation and I am unsure what to do now. Surprise is lost and any further aimless wandering in the enemy's own backyard exposes the team to an unnecessary risk. But I am new to the unit and do not want to create a poor impression on the officers and the men. Reputations matter in a fighting unit. It is the truism of war that the value of no man, howsoever able, is validated until it has been submitted to the ordeal of battle, until his response to the threat of violence is known. I drift around the countryside, circling back and running into a makeshift improvised camp of tarp bivouacs (tarpaulin shelters) with a large drum for water. Clearly, it has been evacuated in a hurry. A quick search produces some old, discarded movie tickets and a discharge receipt from a clinic in Rameshwaram. This was where the LTTE lookout party had been living at the forest edge, keeping me under observation, barely 200 metres from where I had halted. The physical evidence of their presence sends a shiver up my spine. Thirty-six hours later, I roll back to the post to be accosted by the major for insisting on continuing with the operation when surprise was lost.

Even if they may not have endorsed my decision in their hearts of hearts, when quizzed, the officers and the senior JCO (junior commissioned officer) convey in no uncertain terms that as the leader of the team in the field, all decisions are mine and will be backed by the commanders in the rear. The man on the ground is always right, unless proven otherwise. This reminds me of an incident involving Lt Gen Harbaksh Singh, the western army commander during the 1965 Indo–Pak war and the man responsible for the defence of Punjab. During a phase of the war when things were not going too well for the Indians, he received verbal orders from the then Chief, Gen JN Chaudhury, to pull back his troops to the Beas bridge on the GT road. The army commander, however, did the opposite and launched an offensive operation, decisively winning the battle thereafter and altering the course of the war. On being queried why, his reasoning was: 'How could a man who had not made one visit to the frontline to ascertain the situation for himself take such an important decision? It had to be the commander present on the spot.' I rest my case. Experiential knowledge is compelling and necessary in both the planning and execution of any operation or project.

Furthermore, the army has a very structured way of addressing this concept by alternating an officer's service between field and staff postings. So, in any ugly, untoward situation, the commanders at various levels in the hierarchy are able to handle things efficiently, since they would have, at some stage during their service, served in some capacity or the other in that area and would therefore be well versed in the nuances of the terrain and the overall operating environment. This builds understanding and trust between the planners of an operation and its executors.

This kind of command-and-control process and ethic needs to be adopted across the board in every organisation. Just as battlefield demands first-hand intelligence, so too does a business environment require business leaders to step out of the comforts of their offices and understand the reality on the ground. During my later stint in the private sector, I once witnessed the India head of a product the bank was selling go ballistic on a call at his regional head in the east, who was trying to explain some of the problems he was facing, which were rather unique to that region. The India head was a highly qualified man with degrees from the best B-schools in the country, but was loath to move around, meet his team and understand his area of responsibility. He preferred the comfortable confines of his AC room with implicit faith in his academic knowledge. I had been posted in the east while serving in the army and had just come back from a visit in relation to my work. In fact, his regional head had requested me to try and convince his boss about the ground realities when I went back to the corporate office. But I guess that at a certain level of achievement comes an arrogance and belief that you know it all and that results can often be extracted by bullying and hectoring juniors. Well, in this case, as I expected, it could not. As the saying goes, 'many a false step was made by standing still.' Not only did he end up getting insulted by his junior, he was also reminded in no uncertain terms of his lack of knowledge about the market, the competitors' strengths and their way of operating. Instead of being mature enough to accept his folly and take corrective action, he took umbrage at the tone of his junior, turning vindictive and wrecking a first-class team in the bargain. Most of his team members, some of them exceptionally capable, immediately jumped ship to join the competition and went on to become great leaders in their new organisations.

The advantage of knowing your ground, in a lot of ways, is synonymous with knowing your subject. It stands you in good stead when conveying a point to your seniors, especially if it is unpleasant news. They tend to believe you all the more. In a combat situation, of course, if a subunit under your command gets into a tight situation and if physically possible, your first natural reaction is to rush to the site of the encounter and take charge. Perhaps that is your training in the army, or perhaps it is because of the fact that you deal in the business of lives and the lives in question are of the ones who have gone out to face extreme violence and risk on your behest and command.

I knew a commanding officer who once narrated how a subunit of his had suffered a few casualties. On rushing to the encounter site, he discovered the major in charge grappling with the situation, safely ensconced in a comfortable house a couple of kilometres away. He could still recall the rage he had felt and how keen he had been to sack the man on the spot.

However, it is not only in a crisis that terrain knowledge comes handy. There could be occasions when a lack of the same may constrain you in terms of making realistic plans. Let me narrate a small incident to further emphasise my point about the importance of knowing the ground or the market if you are a corporate person, rather than blindly applying your past experiences to a new market or situation.

Years ago, in the mid-1990s, when militancy in the Kashmir Valley was at its peak, the government decided to send a message of normalcy by allowing the Amarnath Yatra to proceed that year. The army took on the bulk of the responsibility to ensure a peaceful pilgrimage for the thousands of devotees who had to trudge up the corkscrew mountain path to the caves—a walk of about 17 kilometres from the roadhead. A team from our unit was hauled in to provide protection and promptly reported to the brigadier in charge. He had just taken over the brigade and was noticeably distraught at having been moved from a cushy peace posting to a highly volatile area.

The brigadier was a high-profile cavalry officer and had done all his service with tanks, practising mobile warfare on a flat, open desert terrain. Clearly, his operational thinking was linear and worked predominantly in the dimensions of large spaces, speed, shock and awe of massed armoured columns.

Throwing a map on the table without any preliminaries, he traced out the path the pilgrims would be taking. While there would be static units dominating the heights, he wanted our boys to walk along on either side of the path in tandem with the pilgrims, all the while keeping out of sight.

'Simple,' he said in all earnestness, 'like flank protection when an armoured column is on the move.'

The team commander had to garner all the patience and civility at his command and draw the brigadier's attention back to the map, pointing out the contours.

'My right column, sir, will first have to go down into the valley and then climb back cross-country 3,000 feet. It will take me a full day. The pilgrims would have long gone by then. And that is just the beginning, since there are vertical cliffs thereafter.'

This is a small example of a leader who had neither served in that terrain nor studied the map properly. Furthermore, he had not made the effort to acquaint himself with the constraints and the severity imposed by high mountains on the bodies of heavily loaded men. This incident with the brigadier not only highlights his poor grasp of the situation, but also underscores one fundamental truth: real knowledge often comes from direct experience.

Ensuring deep experiential learning is not something to be just restricted to the army or the corporate world, but is applicable in almost every aspect of one's life. Before writing my three books, I made the effort to go back to my old hunting grounds and spent time revisiting and reviving old memories and experiences. While I had lived through those momentous events and most of the incidents were etched into my memory, time had erased the sensory details essential for expressing the smell and feel of a place. I believe it made a huge difference to the overall writing and readers have often commented that they felt transported to the place of action and could very easily latch on to concrete images of the geographical descriptions and the fear and the smell of cordite.

In fact, before any military operational plan is made, the first thing the commander will ask for is all the available ground and terrain information. In today's scenario, this could include satellite or air reconnaissance (recon) photos, all-terrain Google Maps, first-hand information gathered by personal experience of having toured or surveyed the ground or by an SF recon patrol keeping the target under observation. Any plan or proposal conceived in the safe and comfortable confines of a room, detached from ground realities, is doomed. Corporations often make plans based on data collected from the ground by third-party vendors or government sources. The point I am trying to nail here is the absolute necessity for leaders to be personally well versed with the ground realities, which enables complete trust in subordinates executing tasks on the ground. So, whether in combat or a boardroom, assumptions based on second-hand information can often lead to disastrous outcomes.

Likewise, first-hand knowledge enables you to distinguish

clearly between fact and fiction being reported upwards and enables you to take timely corrective action if required. 'Genchi Genbutsu' (go and see for yourself), adopted by Toyota Motors, is a great example of the same ethos. It is a core principle followed for efficient manufacturing and serves as a problem-solving methodology. The Japanese, and especially the Toyota company, passionately believe that the essence in understanding any situation is by going to the source or the actual location and getting a first-hand account of the complexity of the problem, rather than relying on second-hand reports or assumptions. This invariably leads to sounder decision-making and effective solutions—the reason why the Japanese have a reputation for quality manufacturing. A prominent case study involving this concept is on the Toyota Sienna Minivan. The sales for the vehicle in the US were falling and a lot of complaints were coming in regarding the performance of the vehicle. The chief engineer, Yuji Yokoya, turned up and personally drove the vehicle across parts of the US, Mexico and Canada to get a first-hand feel of the problems. This led to major changes in the next version of the vehicle that the company launched in North America.

By sending a senior man to the ground to personally experience driving across the continent, Toyota managed to identify the problems. There was noticeably excessive steering drift on rough gravel roads and poor grip on winding roads. Various other features suitable for the American conditions were missing. The improved version of the vehicle, based on his observations, is a perfect example of how problems should be found and addressed through a real-time analysis of the ground situation. To reiterate, first-hand and real-time reviews of ground realities are far more reliable for decision-making than a hundred reports from various second-hand sources.

Furthermore, in my personal experience of operating in combat, both in Sri Lanka and Kashmir, I picked up cues from the environment that are not taught in training schools, which helped me operate more efficiently. If nothing else, it certainly gave me a higher chance of surviving volatile situations. In a couple of ambushes, as I can recall, I took all precautions to hide our presence. Nevertheless, I noticed a slight increase in the pace of a single person crossing our kill zone on a track; if in company, they would resort to talking loudly. I got the impression that perhaps our presence had been detected and it was basic human nature in a hostile environ to convey normalcy with exaggerated posturing. When patrolling in the jungles or sitting in an ambush, if one were tuned into the surroundings, one could sense a sudden deafening silence sometimes. The jungle was suddenly not as lively as before—a clear sign of the presence of a large animal or a foreign body. Likewise, in Kashmir, an empty street—or locals peeping furtively out of their windows or barricading their doors as you entered the street—spoke louder than words of what was in the offing. The opposition was around. These were all hard-earned lessons which one picks up from the ground and incorporates quickly into his fieldcraft—subtle improvisations and nuances that could make the difference between life and death in combat for a soldier. This brings me to an incident showcasing an even more important point about being observant and analytical when on the ground and preparing yourself fully. As Alexander Pope very accurately remarked, 'A little learning is a dangerous thing. Drink deep, or taste not the Pierian spring.'

The snows are melting on the heights of the Shamshabari range, and the infiltration of militants from across the border is expected anytime as per the standard practice followed over the years. One of the launch pads is a few kilometres from the north Lolab Valley, further up the mountain. Tucked into the folds of the mountains, amidst thick deodar forests, lie the two impoverished Gujjar villages of Dharia and Doban. Once the border is crossed, in a day or two, the treks (an infiltrating/exfiltrating group of *mujahideen* in local jargon) descend on the hamlets for rest and recuperation before being assigned to their respective areas of operations in the valley.

A hastily assembled squad of men falls in as I run a last critical check over the dress and other accoutrements necessary for our covert operation. It is called a pseudo-op in the SF parlance, as part of which we are impersonating a militant group. The idea is to land up in the villages and try and contact a real militant party, ideally one which has just crossed over. There are five of us, three Hindus and two local Kashmiri Muslim boys. All of us have gone through some sort of a rudimentary training, but

I fear not enough to pass muster. While the dress, weapons, long hair and flowing beards would pass us off as *mehman* (guest) *mujahid*s or Pakis, the two Kashmiri soldiers would do all the talking.

Taking a long circuitous route, we emerge from the forest as the day begins to fade, just in time for the evening *namaz.* We present ourselves to a couple of village elders with our tale of how, having crossed over, we had gotten separated from our group and convey that any help in uniting us would be rewarded financially. We ask a few questions about the army's presence and their whereabouts. Tea and biscuits are offered and we are invited to join the congregation of the faithful in the small mosque. The response of the locals, to my mind, seems to be quite encouraging and I give them a brief impromptu talk about *jehad.*

While two of us stay outside, on the pretext that we need to keep an eye open for any army patrols, the other three go ahead into the mosque for the *namaz.* So far so good, I think to myself, but the moment the *namaz* is over and people start filing out, I sense a change in the behaviour of the assembly. Gone is the warmth, bonhomie, the excitement and the offers for all the help. Anyway, we spend a day or two and then roll back to the post. A week or so later, with my beard trimmed and in army fatigues and with fresh faces in tow, I climb back up to the village.

I put the usual questions to the villagers if they had any information about militants.

'I have some intelligence that a foreign *mujahid* group was sighted in the village,' I tell them.

'Oh yes,' answers one of them. 'In fact, they offered *namaz* and stayed around for a couple of days. Except,' he continues with a chuckle, 'they were soldiers like you.'

'Really,' I show surprise, 'and how did you figure it out they were soldiers?'

'Simple, *jenab*,' he replied, 'one of them who went in to offer *namaz* did not know how to wash. We do it elbow down and he just washed his hands. Not only that, he also had a thin red string around his wrist like you are wearing.'

It was a perfect case of little knowledge, reflecting poor preparedness, which in our situation could have had dire consequences.

In the end, the desk can only offer you a static snapshot of a complex situation. To leave this view unchallenged can be dangerous. Step away from the comforts of a familiar setting and confront the reality on the ground. Reject the comparative and deceptive safety of making decisions or forming opinions from behind a desk. The real world, when perceived through your own eyes, is often quite different from what you had pictured or understood from afar.

Takeaways

- ***The man in the field is always right—until proven otherwise.*** *Those closest to the action often see what headquarters cannot. Respect their perspective.*

- ***Know your terrain.*** *Whether it is a battlefield or a market, never operate blind. Deep familiarity with the ground is non-negotiable.*
- ***Base your plans on real-time intelligence, not assumptions.*** *Strategies built on outdated or incomplete information are more dangerous than having no plan at all.*
- ***When in doubt, go and see for yourself.*** *Follow the Toyota principle of* Genchi Genbutsu*—get to the source, walk the floor, talk to the people. Clarity lives on the ground, not in PowerPoint slides.*
- ***Half-baked knowledge leads to fully-baked failure.*** *Trust the field. Test your theories. Validate with facts. Then plan.*

FORTUNE FAVOURS THE DISCIPLINED

Do what you should do, when you should do it, whether you feel like it or not.

–Elbert Hubbard

The central idea of the chapter is to emphasise the importance of discipline in achieving goals and how it can even be beneficial in the normal conduct of life. However, it is not very often that one runs into someone who is naturally talented and disciplined enough to pursue their talent. I suppose in that scenario the point I am going to make is redundant. But over the years, I have seen many a talent wasted or not exploited to its full potential because of an absence of discipline. While talent is God-given and a lot of us may not be fortunate enough to have inherited it genetically or naturally, a serious adherent of discipline can bridge the gap between the talented haves and the not-so-talented have-nots significantly. Even for the naturally gifted, it is discipline that transforms talent into lasting achievement. Despite the SF being made up of men who were all volunteers and needed no top-down diktat, a strict training regimen was nevertheless followed. Over time, this created an all-pervading culture where discipline became self-imposed rather than externally enforced. To quote Lord Moran, 'Discipline, control from without, can be relaxed safely when it is replaced by something higher and better, control from within. Discipline can form a habit and the form of habit is regal.'

Soldiers and officers alike took pride in their specialised skills and diligently worked towards improvement. In the pursuit of excellence, it is said that it takes 10,000 hours of training to become a master. The SF, conscious of this fact, realised the importance of repetitive practice until all critical skills and activities became muscle memory. I recall many night training sessions where all one did was to disassemble and reassemble weapons, all timed and conducted in pitch darkness, sometimes with mixed weapon parts. This was a small exercise, but one that can prove hugely important in a firefight at night. Notwithstanding the fact that we in the SF were a handpicked lot, it was our sheer discipline towards training that set us apart from the rest of the army.

On the subject of training, I am reminded of an innocuous remark made years ago in Kashmir by the then CO of the SF unit I had the privilege to serve in, Col Alin Saha, now a brigadier. This was in the sombre aftermath of an operation in which Captain Davinder Jass and a couple of other men lost their lives. The brigadier wistfully reminisced about the events over a call, as I reminded him of what he had mentioned years ago. It was 23 February 2010, another day in the strife-torn valley of Kashmir. In Brig Saha's words:

'At 0445 hrs, I received a message about a firefight with one of my troops operating in Sopore. As was my practice, I at once left for the location. There was concrete intelligence of a high-level meeting of *jehadis* from various militant groups active in the valley—the Lashkar-e-Taiba (LeT), Jaish-e-Mohammad (JM), Hizbul Mujahideen (HM), etc. The unknown, though, was the exact house where it was supposed to take place and the Chinkipura *mohalla,* as you know is a beehive of houses, crisscrossed with a labyrinth of narrow lanes and bylanes. The team commander decided to send out five-man squads, with the task to keep under surveillance the two or three exit and entry points into the locality and, as per plan, begin the search thereafter at first light. The Rashtriya Rifles (RR) and the police had already thrown a wider cordon around the entire area.

'At some stage during the latter part of the night, Captain Jass and his squad approached a large double-storeyed house at the end of a narrow lane. Leaving three men behind, the captain and his buddy decided to go further up the lane for a quick *dekho.* That is when they were engaged with automatic fire from the large house. Probably, as events were stitched together later from the position of the bodies, the buddy was hit first as he was at point and Jass, seeing his buddy collapse, unmindful of his own safety and in true traditions of the Indian Army, rushed forward, engaging and killing the militant who had shot him. It was at this stage that Jass's weapon perhaps malfunctioned. The other militant, noticing a lull in the firing, opened on Jass from the first floor, tossing a few grenades for good measure. Often, I wonder, though it stays in the realms of speculation, what the outcome could have been if only his weapon had not jammed at the crucial moment. I am sure his superior training would have prevailed over his adversary. Captain Davinder Jass unfortunately went to his maker like a soldier. I am glad the army recognised his act of conspicuous gallantry and awarded him a Kirti Chakra (posthumous).

'Anyway, when I arrived, there was complete bedlam, typical of a situation where a considerable number of troops from different units and organisations are involved. Nobody at that stage knew where Captain Jass and his buddy were and he was not picking up his mobile. The grenades had done their damage and the wounded from Jass's squad were pulled in for medical evacuation. To add to the confusion, the corps commander was breathing down my neck for a clearer picture, as someone had leaked to the press that perhaps Captain Jass had been taken hostage. My first order was to roll in my remaining three teams from separate locations and to confine the other troops, the RR and the police to the fringes of the locality as an outer cordon. Come first light on the 24th, I sent out my boys to sweep the *mohalla*. That is when the bodies of our men were discovered sometime in the afternoon, along with the dead militant.

'The search through the day proved futile and the next day, a JCB excavator was commandeered to demolish the large house from where all the firing had ensued. It seemed that in the fog of battle and darkness, either a bunch of militants had escaped the dragnet or there was a hideout in one of the houses nearby. The corps commander instructed me to abort the op, but I insisted on seeing it through. At about noon on the third day of the op, as the JCB's blade hit a part of the debris, like a jack in the box, out popped a dishevelled, begrimed man with a weapon and made a dash for the alley, randomly firing a burst. As you can imagine, it caught everyone by surprise; however, a couple of my boys opened up. He ran in a zigzag fashion, collecting lead all the while and then collapsed at the end of the alley.'

Now, from the anecdote above, I can draw a lot of obvious lessons—leadership of the CO and Jass; camaraderie in crisis; stress management and so on. And I had served with Alin in an operational area in the past and was acquainted with some of the stellar qualities he possesses. But that is not why I have narrated the incident. Just after the episode, a few of us retired officers made a trip to the unit up in Kashmir to show our solidarity with the boys. As the CO narrated the events over a drink in the evening, a remark that he made stayed with me for a long time. Looking at me wistfully, he said,

'The last guy was the man who, in all probability, shot Jass. He gave us a running battle for two days, then lay doggo in some hideout and was buried under the debris thereafter. When the

JCB started clearing the debris, at some stage he popped out after 50 hours; imagine sir, no food, no sleep, no water and he tries to make a run and all the while tries to take a few more of us down in the end. Now, that is the kind of men we need in the SF. Call it survival instinct or commitment to a cause, the moot point is, how can I train and discipline my men better, so that they acquit themselves with the same lethality, in similar circumstances?'

Learning from the opposition despite having suffered loss, I thought, was the hallmark of a great commander and a man with an open mind to new ideas. What had clearly impressed the colonel was the militant's fighting skills and the discipline he exhibited in extremely life-threatening and trying conditions.

Now, discipline and training are deeply intertwined and symbiotic. They strengthen each other. Without discipline, training loses direction, consistency and impact. It is discipline that helps when motivation fades. Likewise, training helps build discipline. Every time we choose to follow a process, with a goal in mind, we strengthen our mind and self-control. Over time, it becomes less about force and more about habit. That is the level of discipline the SF brought to their training. In fact, the training was taken so seriously that they discouraged competitive games. A few officers, I recall, who reported for probation and were Services squash players, were promptly told to take a call—to hang their racquets on the wall and forget the game or go RTU if they were serious about pursuing the sport. And I am stressing on training simply because it has a direct relation to discipline. The degree or the quantum of training a person puts in is directly related to the degree of discipline he brings to it. The harder you train, the more the discipline that is needed. This is because no worthwhile goal which requires learning or improvement of any kind, be it mental or physical, can be achieved in the absence of discipline.

Social scientists who carried out research on discipline concluded that people who accomplished more in life were invariably either naturally disciplined or had imbibed the quality early in life. Most such people that I met were also invariably early risers and indifferent to sleep beyond the necessary bodily requirement. Lord Moran, who studied soldiers in combat during both the First and the Second World Wars, has the following to say on discipline in his book *The Anatomy of Courage*: 'I have turned over in my mind whether it is possible to relax discipline without impairing the soldier's efficiency as a fighting man and I can find only one answer in the story of war. There is nothing in the life of our times to suggest that we can make an exception now with impunity. In a democracy, we need more, not less, discipline, if by discipline we mean self-control.' He of course talks of discipline purely in the context of war—the discipline to obey orders and the discipline to stand firm in the face of life-threatening danger. A soldier's discipline necessary to carry out his tasks in the line of duty is a different kind of discipline and encapsulates other virtues such as courage, camaraderie and esprit de corps, with team training as one of the tools to achieve the Spartan-like qualities of a warrior. I am covering the subject in its broader sense as applicable to the average person in the conduct of his life. But to be disciplined is easier said than done.

My own response to sloth and complacency over the years has been to follow the simple mantra: 'Get up, dress up, show up, the rest will follow.' While climbing in the Annapurna area in Nepal years ago, I asked Kersi, a senior Parsee friend of mine who was in his early eighties, how he stayed so fit. With an incredulous look of how someone could ask such a naïve question, he answered, 'If you do what you did, you will be doing what you do.' He could have easily said that it boils down to discipline to follow a fixed regimen of exercise, regardless of the years rolling by. If you keep doing what you keep doing, then nothing really changes.

Needless to say, age after 50 will retard physical improvement, demotivate a person and render him loath to put in effort. The aim, therefore, is to overcome age-related languor and bash on. I am often surprised to meet a fit person, with an impressive background of physical endeavours in his youth, reasoning that he does things more his age. 'You see, I am 60 now and cannot be doing stuff that I did as a young man.' Absurd reasoning. To paraphrase Mike Tyson, who said, 'Discipline is about doing something you hate, but do it well all the same.' And he stepped into the ring again in his late fifties against a much younger man. So what if he lost. Watching all the videos I could not but admire the man's commitment to training, whatever the motive may have been—money, attention, fame or just a reason to get fighting fit again. Each of us must eventually find that latent reason to tap into—to be roused enough—to get out of one's comfort zone. To give reasons for other people's achievements is, I believe, a way of unaccepting your own inadequacies in achieving your full potential.

Occasionally, I have been confronted by people claiming how difficult it was to start something they have been thinking about for so long, blaming it on a lack of energy. 'One day I will have more time and energy.' The pity is that time never really comes. Other responsibilities and interests promptly follow to fill up that hard-earned time, or life just moves on and your cherished dream is promptly relegated to being just another unaccomplished desire, to be regretted in later life with a nod of the head and a deep sigh of resignation. But action over comfort is not easily achieved. This struggle is deeply rooted in our biology. All living creatures have energy levels that fluctuate with the time of the day or seasons and man is no different. The animal world understands this concept and conducts its activities according to its energy flow.

Similarly, all of us have personal energy cycles. Some function well early and some have their most productive time in the evening or later at night. The same applies to weekdays and months. Most working people hate Mondays for obvious reasons and their productivity improves as the week progresses. I personally handle the cold weather better than the sweltering heat of summer and am the most physically active during the months of winter. Recognising these patterns implies not just self-awareness—it is essential to strategy. You can accordingly plan your activity to the extent possible. If you are the kind who needs some *quiet* time in the morning, guard it against unnecessary distractions. Avoid your mobile, do not plan meetings and defer important decisions during that phase. Productivity is at its best when it is in consonance with your mind and body mechanism.

However, such flexibility was not a luxury afforded in the SF. Considering the unpredictable and uncertain nature of SF work (24x7x365), it required a different approach. The SF understood human frailty well and devised ways to train men to enable them to adapt rapidly to disruptions in their personal energy cycle, or for that matter any kind of disruption. They loved to mess with your circadian rhythms to build resilience through adaptation. The circadian rhythms govern our bodies in a 24-hour cycle and respond to the stimuli of light and darkness. The most common circadian rhythm is sleep. Your body naturally tends to feel sleepy at night and is more active during daylight. This likewise affects body temperature, alertness, digestion and hormone production in varying degrees—just the thing the SF love to play with. Accordingly, one of the things they followed religiously, as part of their training curriculum, was a month-long phase where all training that would usually happen during the day was shifted entirely to night. This was termed a *commando cycle*. The idea was to break your biomechanics. When the entire battalion was falling in for PT in the morning, you would see a weary bunch of men making their way back to the billets.

The first few days were always miserable; but then, in a brief time, the body adapted to the change and by the end of the cycle, was operating at full productivity, despite the unnatural conditions. It is not something I would recommend for the average person, but it offers a powerful lesson—how discipline is a state of mind and becomes a lifetime habit if built in adversity. This is because when energy and motivation falter, as they often do, it is discipline that carries you forward. And in doing so, it nurtures the very qualities essential for success: perseverance, commitment, stamina and self-confidence.

The US Navy SEALs have a saying, 'Only yesterday was easy.' In other words, every day is a struggle if one must keep improving. Personally, I find running to be extremely hard and yet, from time to time, I have signed up for some ultramarathon or the other. On many an occasion for assorted reasons, one struggles to quit the bed early in the morning for the run. As a rule, I follow my mantra and show up, since experience has taught me that a run is never as hard as it seems at the start line. And that is the reason I get the maximum satisfaction from running, because it is so hard for me. Invariably, anything that comes easily in life is rarely appreciated. Have I improved my running over the years, especially with age creeping in? The answer is no. But I have certainly managed to significantly retard the deterioration that comes with age and injury at times. There are also times when I just stand around, do some stretches or go for a walk. A wasted effort. But that's where discipline begins, not with performance, but by presence. That is the first rule of discipline; it demands your physical presence at the place of action. While I harp about discipline in relation to physical labour, the same principles apply equally to someone pursuing intellectual or mental goals.

Discipline, while a personal trait, leads to institutional/organisational excellence when present in a body of men with a shared goal. That is the aim and focus all SF units strive for. Ram Charan highlights execution as the core element of any organisation's culture and it is a *discipline* integral to its strategy. He further asserts that execution is both a discipline and a system, is not only about tactics and must be built into a company's culture, strategy and goals.

The question, therefore, that begs attention is that if discipline were so easy, then would not everybody achieve great heights? So, what is discipline? One of the definitions explains it as training oneself to do something in a controlled and habitual way. This is possible through self-control. And self-control is a mental game. The only common advice I recall being given to me by all and sundry during my selection was that '*Commando, sahib, goday mein nahin, dimaag mein hai*' (A commando is not defined by his knees/body; it is his mind that makes him one). And this belief, cast in stone, was communicated in the unit by word of mouth from generation to generation, especially during probation or in times of relentless stress. Discipline, therefore, is directly a by-product of the mind and a feeble mind will invariably resist any attempts at self-control, especially where it entails discomfort that comes from stepping out of the comfort zone. The mind clearly in the SF had more relevance than the body and for them was the *axis mundi,* from where originated all strength, control, willpower, etc.

With so much emphasis on the mind, it was inconceivable that the SF would not have a theory around strengthening the same. And because a large bulk of the work entails extreme physical stress, they came to a simple conclusion: the mind grows through suffering. In fact, this belief perhaps applied to the entire army and was followed in some form or the other across the board. In the military academy, for example, a very crucial role of strengthening the cadets is played by the seniors, in what is unambiguously called 'fuck sessions'. It involves off-work hour extra physical *ragada* or exercise, doled out for any number of reasons as a form of group or individual punishment. For all the front-rolling and back-rolling and running and other vicious ways to disgorge the food that one had consumed, what really messed with my head was a simple alternation between standing and lying positions, getting back up and repeating for an hour or so, with a pack filled with gravel. The worst was not the intensity—it was the monotony. As we all know, repetitive activity can be boring, monotonous and mind-numbing, but in my experience incredibly beneficial—beneficial in certain skill-based disciplines. It is not just about muscle—it builds mental resilience.

And it taught me something I see echoed in high-performing

corporate workplaces today: growth is not always dramatic. It doesn't only come in strategy sessions or big presentations. Often, it is built in the quiet grind—reworking a proposal for the fifth time, showing up at a 7 AM call when no one is watching, sitting with discomfort instead of outsourcing it. Whether in uniform or in business, resilience is not forged during the easy wins—it is built in the dull, demanding, repetitive moments that test your patience more than your performance.

Consistency under pressure is what sets professionals—and organisations—apart. I saw this again during my combat diving course with the navy. Like in the SF, the culture at the diving school was machismo. One particular test required us to sit still, with full diving gear, on the seabed, doing nothing. An hour is a long time with no task to occupy your mind. I would slow down everything—breathing, thinking, meditating, observing curious little fish and so on. However, there is a limit to beguiling your own mind and from time to time you had this strong urge to rip off the face mask and surface. We would beg the instructors to give us any work, clean the ships in the docks, weld something—anything to keep at bay the tedium that comes with inactivity. Their answer was standard: it makes your mind strong. Guess they knew something with experience that the uninitiated like us were ignorant of: 'What doesn't kill you makes you stronger.'

The same lesson was reinforced in Sri Lanka, except that the inactivity here was performed in a bush, since most of our operations were carried out in the jungle lying in ambush and at times from 48 to 72 hours. For a healthy young man that is an exceedingly long time to remain immobile. There is merit in the saying, 'That it is only from the point of view of stillness that one understands motion.' Try explaining that to a fit young man. It is only in hindsight that one understands the benefits. It takes an enormous amount of self-control to remain static for so long. Needless to say, the Tamil Tigers were good teachers to ensure you quickly learnt the wisdom of staying still. The Aghori babas have a practice of burying their heads in sand in a head stand position. What is the point you will ask? Well, according to them, it strengthens the mind.

The ancient Stoics had their own way of teaching this—they suggested setting aside a few days, now and then, during which one should be content with the plainest of food and truly little of it, and wear rough coarse clothing and then ask oneself, 'Is this what one used to dread?' Quite a different concept, but with the same purpose—to prepare the mind for hardship and to the transient nature of life, where both happiness and sorrow are fleeting and invariably one follows the other.

Research has shown that suffering, whether physical, emotional or psychological, activates certain brain systems. The anterior cingulate cortex (ACC) detects conflict and pain—both physical and emotional—and a repeated activation of the same leads to an enhanced coping mechanism. It manages distress and resists impulsive responses. The prefrontal cortex inhibits impulsive responses and exerts willpower. Suffering can strengthen these circuits when we choose to endure, adapt or learn from it—a process called 'effortful control'.

So, whether through repetition or stillness, the idea is the same—to strengthen/prepare the mind. While repetitive action to hone a certain skill is understandable, stillness, bordering on complete inactivity, to strengthen the mind seems a bit far-fetched. But then it is inertia with a purpose. To quote Seneca, 'A persevering steadfastness of purpose counts for a lot, so that even inertia if stubbornly maintained may carry a certain weight.' The ancient Indians, cognisant of the dominance of the mind in the conduct of life, discovered meditation, the benefits of which need no enumeration here. Mind control leads to self-control and self-control leads to a disciplined life. In other words, the three are synonymous.

Years later, the benefits of this learning came back to me quite inadvertently. After leaving the army, I took part in a few ultramarathons across the world. These were seriously long distances, on an average 250 kilometres spread over 6 days across varied terrain. The breed of ultra-runners often referred to themselves as the pain community, and a quote by Murakami, who was himself a distance runner, very succinctly sums up the essence of ultra-running, 'Pain is mandatory, but suffering is optional.' But that optionality exists only if your mind is strong. And this suffering can only be endured if the mind can transcend discomfort. I share the ultra-experience for two reasons. The first is that physical suffering helps to strengthen the mind by giving you the confidence to go through adversity, apart from building trust and faith in your mental powers that are essential to encourage you to keep raising the bar in your future undertakings. 'Adversity', as an anonymous wise man said, 'introduces a man to himself.' This incidentally was also one of the positive fallouts of having undergone an SF selection process. Not only were you exposed with all your strengths and weakness to the selectors, but also came out of it a much wiser man about yourself. It peeled away the layers and stripped you naked in front of yourself. You learnt things about yourself which you would never have discovered in your normal life. You came out raw, stripped of illusions, but wiser.

The second reason is to illustrate how a well-trained mind can compensate for physical unpreparedness, especially when directed towards a specific purpose. The few of us from the SF who took part in these races, all in their late forties and early fifties, were conscious of their unpreparedness for the gruelling race. All of us were busy juggling our respective careers after leaving the army. In my case, living in Mumbai, the city that had neither the conducive weather nor the space to train for an endurance event, other than a paucity of time, made it worse. But what we all had in common and in abundance was a rich background spent in the SF. We had tested our bodies and minds and knew what they were capable of. That became our anchor. And on that premise, half the distance was done on the training we had put in and the other half we were confident could be completed on sheer willpower. Like the old days in the SF, the mind was to be put to the test. The ability to bear extreme discomfort and suffering was given and accepted as a part of the experience. This is not a strategy I would recommend to the average person, since any endeavour demands a certain basic level of preparation, mental or physical, the neglect of which can impact the outcome drastically.

The last long run, however, was when I was fifty-four; it was a 265-kilometre mountain ultra in Spain. I went with the usual belief—partly in my training and the rest in a tenacious willpower to see me through. However, I was, to my surprise, utterly wrecked to say the least. Somewhere age had caught up and the mind was diminished in its capacity to take punishment, and as a consequence, the degree of suffering overwhelmed the mind's ability to negate the effects. Detaching the latter from the bodily fatigue and pain became not only distressing but also quite intractable. Negative thoughts were clouding the mind and the constant chatter in the head was directing me to abandon the run. The fourth day was a long run of 60 kilometres with nearly half the distance on a steep incline. With swollen feet and arms, somewhere midway I sat down, succumbing to the defeatist little voices of gloom in my head. If it was not for this friend from the SF, Dalip Bhalla, who went past taking a dig at my pitiable attitude, I would probably still be sitting there! I realised that day that the mind, like the body, needs to be exercised regularly. It was Churchill I think who said, 'If you are going through hell, keep going.'

With so much emphasis on fitness, it would be amiss of me

not to briefly touch on what really constituted fitness in the SF. The global state of physical inactivity, especially in India, is alarming. The facts are troubling enough for this physical inactivity to be termed a 'silent killer'. According to *The Lancet*, a medical journal, a combined analysis of 507 surveys across 162 countries revealed that as much as a third of the global population and half of India's adults did not meet the WHO-recommended standards of physical activity. That is one in every two adults in this country!

Anyway, to quote Myers, 'You are fit if you can adapt to the demands of your environment with ease and imagination.' And the demands in the SF were very stiff. Fitness was not about what it is considered now—pushing weights and bulking up, for when it comes to real strength and self-defence, muscle power is not the path. The Indian Army, for recruits and cadets in its training schools/academies, perhaps followed a Swedish form of exercise called Fartlek, which was basically developed in the late 1930s for middle and distance runners. To that, they threw in their own set of functional training to improve strength, flexibility, balance and suppleness.

As a university man who was into building a body, the concept of endurance came as a bit of a shock to me when I joined the army. While strong of the upper body, my first 1-mile run at the OTA (officers' training academy) was done in a miserable 7 minutes. And as the runs progressed and the miles added up, I hated to see my muscles gradually shrink, till realisation dawned what the concept of fitness meant in consonance with my job as an SF soldier. The SF clearly followed the view of natural and functional training, advocated by various eminent physicians and athletes through the ages and then layered it with extreme endurance. All physical training in the end was designed to enable a man to lug heavy weights over long distances in any terrain and weather.

To this, I may add a paucity of sufficient calories for the physical labour that the task may entail. Compared to the food we consume today and the availability of high-calorie stuff like gels, bars, etc., that I have often carried for my endurance races, I am surprised how we managed such extreme physical toil on a daily basis, on a diet mostly of two eggs, rice, *chapatti* and potatoes. In fact, the men's cookhouse practically had only *puri* and potato *sabji* every day for breakfast. And the latter constituted our field rations too when out on operations. A small portion of chicken was thrown in, perhaps twice or thrice a week. It goes without saying that the army authorities had worked out a minimum healthy, nutritious diet necessary for an average soldier. Reckon they slipped up in figuring out separately a diet for the SF, where the average calorie burn and the daily existence were akin to attending an athletic camp in preparation for a major championship.

Now I mention diet here to highlight the point that the human body is capable of delivering under extreme physical challenges on very little food. I am talking about endurance and not muscle building. It is a mindset I notice today, especially amongst the youngsters, to load more calories than is necessary. Protein shakes and supplements, it seems, have replaced the good old glass of milk. Needless to say, I make this statement for the average person, who perhaps throws in an hour of gym, runs or walks six days a week. I am also conscious when I make this statement, that no formal structured study was ever carried out in the unit, where perhaps a group of us given a better high-protein diet may have outperformed the others. But too much food, clearly out of proportion with the physical exertions, seems to be a bane of modern society and reflects quite noticeably in the rising scourge of obesity.

Edwin Checkley, a physician and an athlete, in his book on the natural methods of physical training in 1880, thrashed the idea of diets, muscle building and circuit training and focused on real-world stuff instead. Hard muscle and stiff strength were not considered the true measure of real fitness. He wrote, 'You feel the muscle expanding. Those biceps especially draw attention, as if they were the synonyms of health and strength. The strength of the man so trained has no reliance on itself. It is superficial—skin deep, as it were—and will not stay put.'

Most visitors to our SF unit were often disappointed to see the men, having formed an opinion about their physical stature from the numerous Hollywood movies. For most of them were sinewy or sparsely built, with sunken cheeks and chests. Unless one had seen them in action, it was difficult to fathom how they could lug heavy weights and endure severe physical punishment.

Checkley believed his natural training done mostly outdoors

gave everything—shape, speed, strength, suppleness, endurance, abounding health and every blessed advantage a man can have. Georges Hebert, a Frenchman, followed up on the same precept, calling his fitness regimen the *methode naturelle* and based it on a philosophy he termed *être fort pour être utile*—be fit to be useful. It recognised three basic components for useful fitness: physical training: heart, lungs and muscles—to include dexterity, endurance, resistance and balance; mental training: energy, will power, courage, coolness and firmness; and ethical behaviour: friendship, collective work and altruism. The above could have easily been written as a fitness manual for an elite operations unit.

Years ago, I once asked Brigadier FFC Bulsara, one of the early pioneers of the Indian SF and later famous as the commander of the Maldives operation, as to what he considered fitness. Recovery, he said, was the ultimate test of fitness—the ability to repeat a physical test at the earliest. Renowned for his physical strength and fondly addressed as Bull in the Parachute Regiment, he reminisced that as a young officer, he could run a 2-mile test or the obstacle course in excellent timing and then repeat it again in excellent time with a 10-minute rest in between. Anybody who has run the 2-mile test in the old days will tell you that even to pass, one had to exert. I found there was much merit in what the seasoned brigadier had said.

While timing for the various mandatory runs was an oft-repeated discussion amongst the men and officers, the place of pride went to the guys who had the reputation to carry weight over distance. I recall an operational discussion for a trans-border raid somewhere in the far east of the country. The packed rucksacks with the battle loads were lined up, and a typical no-holds-barred discussion was on, with the men's opinion being sought on the overall planning. The major commanding at some stage asked Rohtas, a hard-bitten, big-built Jat who had earned his place amongst the fittest in the unit, the distance one could reasonably hope to cover at night.

The man picked up the heaviest rucksack, took a step or two, wiped the sweat of his brow, for the weather was muggy like a sauna and then, looking at the major, answered, 'Considering the ammo you are suggesting we carry *sahib,* the atrocious weather, slushy paddy fields and a night march, I can throw in a maximum of 15 km.'

That was the end of the planning. If Rohtas could handle just 15 km and the same distance back, with a fight to be considered in between, then clearly we were stretching our capabilities. This background of extreme endurance, often bordering on masochism, became the basic foundation for fitness for a lot of us. Guess it was the reason why quite a few of us, even after quitting the army, went about taking part in tough ultramarathons, climbs and solo cycling expeditions. There is no satisfaction derived from exercise till such time the heart rate is pushed up and the lungs are made to gasp for air, or long enough for the mind to be exerted in the endeavour of the physical activity. Most of my important decisions and planning for the day are done while running. The long runs, especially, are a great time to connect with yourself, more so if it is a trail run. Nothing like the outdoors, for researchers studying the effect of nature had the following observation to make, 'A simple and brief interaction with nature can produce a marked increase in cognitive control.'

Patrick Leigh Fermour, an English writer, scholar and soldier, who wrote some remarkable travelogues, had a motto—*solvitur ambulando*—when in doubt, walk. An echo of that viewpoint still resonates with us—very appropriate to cater to the hustle and bustle of the modern world, ie, to walk a minimum of 10,000 steps every day. I recall that when I was working, most of the HR departments in companies across the board had a 10,000-step-a-day competition to ensure employees stayed fit. But having said that, often when I see someone with an impressive physique, for a fleeting moment, I lament the loss of a great body that I could have perhaps had.

Be it the SF or any other civilian profession, success comes from consistent, often arduous practice of self-control and persistence. While fitness in the SF is of an extreme construct, it is in consonance with the nature of the job. Any level of fitness has a direct relation to the discipline one brings to achieve it. Let hardship sharpen your resolve and remember, it is the rigorous application of discipline that ultimately sets apart the achiever from the non-achiever. So, stand up, dress up and show up.

Takeaways

- ***Discipline is not a trait—it is a habit.*** *It compounds quietly over time, until the results speak for themselves.*
- ***Repetition builds mastery.*** *Especially in skill-based domains, disciplined repetition lays the foundation for excellence.*
- ***Empirical studies back it up.*** *High performers consistently display higher levels of self-discipline and self-regulation.*
- ***Success often wakes early.*** *The majority of accomplished individuals maintain structured routines, including moderate and consistent sleep habits.*
- ***Keep showing up.*** *Stay the course. Raise the bar when you can—but never step backwards.*
- ***Know your rhythm.*** *Align work with your natural energy cycles; discipline is not about burning out, but working smart.*
- ***Resilience forged in adversity lasts longer.*** *Discipline built under pressure creates depth and staying power.*
- ***Detach from outcomes. Commit to the process.*** *As the Bhagawad Gita reminds us: 'Do your duty, but do not concern yourself with the results.'*
- ***In any organisation, execution is everything.*** *And execution is a direct outcome of a culture rooted in discipline.*
- ***Discipline begins in the mind.*** *And the mind, like muscle, can be trained. Strengthen it and you strengthen everything.*

- ***Hardship builds capability.*** *The body and mind grow through controlled suffering. Excess comfort, food and ease create fragile performers.*
- ***Performance is sustained output.*** *Modern fitness chases appearance; the Special Forces trained for repeatable performance under fatigue, load and uncertainty. If it can't be sustained, it doesn't count.*

NO TASK WITHOUT A GOAL

When a task has to be completed, hesitate not to call a donkey your father.

–An old Hindustani saying

I was a few months into my service and still unfamiliar with the culture in an SF unit. The senior major summoned me one hot sultry day and explained the 36-hour ambush operation to be carried out that night. The grid reference he pointed out on the map was a place I had patrolled a couple of weeks back. While the map showed a lively green colour indicating a forest, in reality there were fallow open fields with no cover whatsoever. This was Sri Lanka and a small body of men seen in the open for a lengthy duration of time was a temptation the Tamil Tigers would be hard-pressed to ignore. Forget about laying an ambush, we ran the risk of getting bushwhacked ourselves. The hesitancy in my expression must have been discernible, since the major gave me a sharp look which needed no words. I promptly decided to hold my counsel.

I stepped out nodding my head in confusion and muttering something under my breath. The senior JCO noticed my discomfiture and walked up to me. I blurted out the orders received and mentioned that he had been with me on the last excursion and knew the risks involved. The man heard me out and in chaste Haryanvi quoted an old Hindustani saying, 'In the SF, *sahib*, when a task is to be completed, hesitate not to call a donkey your father. Once the task is done, if you so desire, ride the damn beast. You should have expressed your concerns when the orders were given, but once you have accepted to do the job, well, switch your mind to how it must be accomplished rather than wasting time mulling over the impossibility and the unfairness of the task.'

This lesson, delivered with brutal simplicity, underscored the central tenet of our ethos: executing a task matters primarily, apart from conveying the organisation's professional culture. Accomplishing goals was a way of life, a given and no excuses would be tolerated for floundering or failure. The nature of the job in the SF involves high-intensity, high-risk and low-duration operations. As we do not hold ground like normal infantry, all jobs are task-oriented. The non-accomplishment of a task was viewed very seriously and a failure led to a lot of soul-searching and introspection at all levels. Drills, procedures, methodology, equipment and even leadership came under intense scrutiny and people were often sacked, regardless of rank, for an error in judgment or delinquency in proper and expected standards of conduct.

The tasks in the army and the SF were specific and measurable, with unambiguous accountability and ownership. Rewards and punishment were similarly immediate and linked. In contrast, in the corporate world, I often saw highly qualified managers who were brilliant at strategising and conceptualising, but had zero idea, interest or competence at execution. A flair for presentation and articulation finesse had propelled them up the ladder. I once reported to an English guy, on two separate occasions and in two different companies, who had managed to hold important positions across several south-east Asian country offices purely due to his presentation strength and smooth talking and in those days, had the advantage of his skin colour too. He would of course promptly jump companies before he could be held accountable for all the deliverables he had promised. But you cannot fool everyone all the time and his reputation started preceding him soon, with doors getting shut.

Time is a critical dimension of value. Every goal carries a shelf life—miss the window and the reward often loses its meaning. Consider a simple example: if your goal was to buy a car at thirty, but delays push that milestone to fifty, the gratification is not the same. The joy is not just in *what* we achieve—but *when* we do it.

Every task, regardless of its scale, has two essential pillars: planning and execution. This holds true whether you are in a boardroom, launching a product or leading troops through hostile terrain. A solid plan without timely action is like a map with no one to walk the path.

And yet, in my experience—across corporates and even within the armed forces—execution often becomes the neglected stepchild of planning. We obsess over strategy decks, flowcharts and brainstorming sessions, but when it is time to pull the trigger, many hesitate. I have seen individuals—brilliant, capable ones—become paralysed by the sheer weight of the task. Over-analysis morphs into inertia. Meetings multiply, but movement stalls.

This tendency is not just an organisational flaw—it is a cultural one—a sort of national allergy to timely execution. We plan, we revise, we polish, but we delay.

What is the antidote to this? It is an action bias. In high-performance environments, clarity is not enough. Timeliness is non-negotiable. Execution is a skill, a mindset, a muscle—and like all muscles, it must be trained.

There are of course sudden crises situations that may arise in combat and need on-the-spot decisions that may either affect the overall outcome of a battle, or in the case of a minor skirmish in an insurgency scenario, get more kills. In either case, your men's lives are at stake. In such situations, a cool clear mind is necessary, with an ability to quickly grasp the unfolding events and decisively execute. A person can be trained for these high-pressure situations by simulating hypothetical scenarios and creating the stress that it entails by crunching the response time. Global companies and even governments often carry out this crisis management exercise to test the decision-making ability of the leaders and the response time of the teams executing the instructions on the ground.

But at the heart of it, it is a person's natural temperament that often determines how calmly and effectively they respond to a crisis. Training, systems and protocols matter—but in the moment, it is temperament that takes the wheel.

I have often witnessed this play out in a corporate crisis that mirrored battlefield chaos. The MD wants something asap and the line manager presses the panic button. The team disintegrates as individuals start pushing blame up and down the chain. Chaos brews. That is when a leader needs to calm things down and focus the team back to the task. The product may not be perfect, but good enough to avoid disaster.

I have seen a similar temperament in field commanders—bombs going off, radios crackling, men shouting—and yet the best leaders (an ex-commanding officer of mine comes to mind) speak less, move slower and think clearer. Their calm becomes contagious. Panic spreads fast. But so does composure. And while experience helps, temperament—the ability to stay grounded under pressure—is the difference between reacting and responding, between collapse and control.

An approach of breaking down the mission into clear

measurable steps not only minimises risk and failure, but also ensures accountability at every level and corrective action. Efficient people set themselves daily/weekly and annual goals. In the army they taught you to break a task into three components at a basic level: manpower required, timelines for completion and the tools/hardware the job needed or available. Later, in my corporate innings, another dimension got added—the cost involved for the overall project. In the army it was return on effort mostly, with returns being weighed against loss of lives, while in the corporate world a return on investment is purely based on financials. The breaking down of the main goal into smaller tasks can then be measured and monitored weekly, monthly or quarterly for both the team in question and separately for the individuals that make up that team. This gives the leader a chance to tweak the plan if needed or weed out or interchange individuals who may not be suited for the job they had been assigned. The plan must have built-in adaptability and agility. Adapting is key to survival for any business, especially in a rapidly evolving environment which requires you to pivot quickly to a changing market and not get drawn into overcommitting resources and money to a plan that is failing.

In my time in the corporate world, other than the department goals, I would go a little further with my team. I would impress upon the team members to get back with some of their personal goals for the year. It could be anything—run 5 kilometres, start a blog or anything mundane which they had been thinking about for some time, but never really got down to committing it to action. And these would be reviewed by me for sure at the time of the annual appraisals. This was my way of trying to inculcate in them a habit to develop interest and hobbies and gently coerce them to take time off to pursue the same. Personally, for years, other than my department goals, I would write down my personal goals under the three headings—academic, financial and physical, that is, write something, a book, a column etc; investments and savings for the year; and finally for the latter, a race or a swim or any other outdoor activity. Life is meaningless without goals.

Albert Camus and Jean-Paul Sartre, two leading thinkers of existentialism and absurdism, explored the question of whether life has any real meaning in a world that often seems hostile and uncaring. They believed life has no built-in purpose—it is, in a sense, absurd. Yet, they also believed that to live fully, we must still find or create our own goals, even if that seems contradictory. For both, the core idea is simple: life may be meaningless, but we must still choose to live with purpose.

For both thinkers, the paradox is clear: life is meaningless, yet we must create or embrace meaning to live authentically. Also, life is meaningless, yet we must embrace the absurd, live without appeal and find value in the struggle. Sartre believed in creating meaning through free choices and committing to endeavours that reflect your own goals and values.

In my experience—whether you are in the middle of a firefight or chasing down a business target—success hinges on three non-negotiables: clear task orientation, a shared understanding of stakeholder expectations and a realistic definition of what success looks like.

Let me break it down.

First, unambiguous task orientation means everyone on the team knows *exactly* what the mission is. Not vaguely, not 'kind of'—but precisely. What needs to be done, by whom and by when. Without this clarity, even the most talented teams will drift.

Second, stakeholder alignment is crucial. In both combat and corporate settings, there are always multiple parties involved—team members, managers, clients, commanders and partners. If their expectations are not understood and managed, frustration builds and momentum breaks down.

And third, you need a clear, shared sense of success. Are we aiming for survival, growth, market share, efficiency or innovation? If success is not clearly defined, you might cross the finish line only to find it was not the right race.

Whether bullets are flying or numbers are sliding in a boardroom, these three elements form the foundation of any successful operation.

Ask questions without hesitation. If you are not clear about the goal as a leader, your subordinates certainly cannot be expected to pull in the right direction in unison. At the risk of not looking like a fool, people often shy away from inquiring. While I hesitated to raise my hand and ask for clarification during my schooling and college, my approach changed drastically once I joined and gained experience in the SF. The nature of the job dictated complete clarity to the extent possible, for experience had taught us that in the fog of combat, things would invariably go awry, stranding you in a situation for which you should have sought the answers before you initiated action. In my corporate career, my response when being given a task was to request my superior to explain it to me, like he would to a ten-year-old child. Everybody's grasping power differs and it often helps if you break down the instruction into its nuts and bolts.

Clarifying the details of a task is essential, even if it means challenging a superior respectfully, since clarity is not just about asking questions, it is also about having the moral courage to express disagreement when something does not sit right with you. In both the army and the civilian professions, the skill to articulate uncertainty and demand clarity not only protects against costly errors but also builds trust within the team. In your professional life, these situations will invariably arise, where you may, in varying degrees, disagree on a certain point with your superior. It could be on moral or ethical grounds, or a decision could just seem unsound or unprofessional. If you are convinced and feel strongly about it, do not hesitate to express your reservation. Learn to say no. How it needs to be conveyed, considering the human egos at play, has been covered later in the chapter. Needless to say, it was far more difficult a task in the army than it is in civilian professions. And I have experienced both the worlds. I paraphrase Lord

Moran, who believed that 'moral courage was far more noble and difficult an attribute to possess, than physical courage.' In certain circumstances, to say no, which may be morally the right thing, is a far more difficult proposition than a yes.

Military history is replete with examples of armies failing because the commander did not have the moral courage to speak his mind during the planning stage. A powerful example of how things can go disastrously wrong without clarity is the famous Charge of the Light Brigade during the Crimean War.

The Light Brigade was a group of elite British cavalry. They received an order to charge—but the order was vague and poorly communicated. Instead of seeking clarification, Lord Cardigan, who was leading the brigade, acted on a misunderstood version of the order and led his men straight into a valley surrounded by Russian artillery—a suicidal charge. The Light Brigade galloped head-on into cannon fire, following orders, simply because the chain of communication was muddled and no one stopped to clarify the orders received. If your team misunderstands your direction, if stakeholders are not aligned, or if you rush ahead without clarifying the goal—you may be charging bravely...but in the wrong direction. Mistakes grow in the space where clarity is missing.

Never confuse urgency with clarity. Take a moment. Ask the hard questions. Ensure everyone is aligned. Because a few extra seconds of clarity can save years of regret and hard work and in the army, lives.

While history instructs, personal experience teaches and reinforces. Be conscious of the viability of a task or job before accepting it. It is essential to be certain that the goal is achievable, since it is pointless to accept a task when your mind is riddled with uncertainties of it ever coming to fruition. Such a task is doomed for failure from the inception. I had my own brush with poor articulation once, where my well-meaning but blunt statement nearly derailed my standing and reputation. Having been brought up by a father who instilled the virtues of straight talk, I learnt the hard way in the army on how to disagree or put across my point of view in a diplomatic manner. As a young captain, I once vented my views in a commanders' conference, where operational deployment was being discussed and I was slated to take the team up to Kashmir. I thought the boys needed more training before being thrown into a highly volatile combat area. I therefore informed the brigadier (not requested, mind you, as service etiquette dictated) about the need for more preparation time and a postponement of my departure.

'Why do you need it?' he asked.

In hindsight, I should have been more careful with my verbalisation. What I blurted out was that my men were not fit for war and I could guarantee casualties if dispatched in a hurry. Now, you do not make that sort of a statement in a professional army which is meant to be always in readiness for any exigency, especially in the SF. Wars and emergencies never really come with adequate preparation time to meet them.

You could have heard the proverbial pin drop and then the brigadier exploded at the gumption of a young captain to stand up and say something like that to a senior brigadier in the presence of so many officers, including his commanding officer. What I spoke was all truth, but put across incompetently. Men being unfit for war and the need for postponement of departure not only reflected poorly on the competence of the CO but could also have been construed as an attempt to shirk combat. Needless to say, I had to seek a private interview with the brigadier later to apologise and explain my lack of nuance in conveying what I meant.

There were other times when verbalising resistance came with real consequences, showing how disagreement, if not framed correctly, can decide not just career trajectories but also your immediate survival.

We are in the middle of a memorable mission near the Indo-Myanmar border. Two SF teams from different battalions are tasked to raid a Naga insurgent camp a few kilometres across the border in Myanmar, then called Burma. One team sits on the border as a cut-off force for any insurgents who may scatter after the fireworks start, while our team gets the task of raiding the camp. A captured National Socialist Council of Nagaland (NSCN) insurgent, who knows about the camp, guides us across savage mountain country in the most enervating muggy weather. As we hit the thick jungle on the ridge line, it starts to drizzle. It is a 12-hour climb to the border, weighed down with all the accoutrements of war and under constant threat of an ambush, since the men sitting on the border are intercepting insurgent chatter on the radio about the possibility of ambushing us. This conversation is getting relayed to us in real time and other than slowing down our speed, is also amplifying the overall stress levels.

It is a steep uphill climb, heavily forested and every couple of steps one must stop, scan the surroundings and do a listening drill—all very time-consuming. The night is spent on a narrow game trail, with our legs hanging over a *nala* gushing with rainwater. The squad in the vanguard gets separated and ends up engaging imaginary Naga militants in the darkness, or perhaps they sight movement. Nobody is sure and it turns out to be the mother of all nights. The next morning, the party presses on despite having lost surprise. Anyway, the camp is reached, the rocket launchers engage and the raiding party exchanges fire with a lone militant tasked with chopping wood. The camp is empty. And, it is the most elaborate and beautiful camp one can imagine in the back of beyond, with a church, badminton court, separate quarters for the seniors and barracks with running water. All of this is made from teakwood and bamboo, which were freely available and the entire camp is camouflaged under the thick canopy of the forest.

A second night out is spent in the camp and we trudge back the next day. Nobody has the heart to destroy anything made with so much labour and love. And I still wonder what happened to the camp, since the Nagas, as a practice, never go back to a camp which has been compromised. Anyway, it is another long day of slogging and by the time we board the vehicles at the Dogra post, it is late in the evening. It has been 48 hours of no sleep and practically no food and everybody is bone-tired, dozing away as the vehicles wind up the road to Ukhrul. Suddenly, in a place called Shangshak, where in 1944 the British Indian Army's Parachute Brigade fought a grim battle and delayed the Japanese from reaching Kohima, we are waylaid and told to report to the brigade HQ.

There is heightened activity, everybody is in uniform and the brigade HQ is buzzing, with people dashing about seemingly on important errands. We are directed to the ops room and received by a colonel who is the deputy commander. The two team commanders, both majors, sit in front and the rest of us flop down in the chairs behind and promptly doze off. We are jolted out of our slumber with a command to attention as the brigade commander breezily makes his entry in full battle gear. I do not recall any introductions being made, as the commander picks up the pointer stick and launches verbally into the crisis of the moment. Apparently, an infantry battalion under his command has been hit and they have 7–8 dead on their hands. The commander is in a foul mood and wants immediate retribution—eye for an eye, blood for blood. It strikes me that while we were busy hitting one of their camps, the insurgents had been elsewhere, squaring the account.

The commander, in his hour of crisis, must have made the calls to the right quarters and been informed that he was in luck, for two SF teams were operating in his area. 'Hallelujah,' what better than to waylay the lot and unleash them back into the bush. We had already figured out what was afoot and whispered to the team commanders to bail us out. We were a spent force. With a flourish of his pointer, the commander wrapped up his op orders. While we made a pretence of listening, I doubt if any of us had heard what he had said. Wriggling out of this one was clearly going to need deft handling. Our team commander, who was the senior of the two majors and just back from the prestigious Staff College course, cleared his throat and stood up.

'No problem, sir. We will go in the moment we have replenished food and ammo. Just one slight problem, sir. Not sure if you are aware that we are reporting straight to the MO (Military Operations) in Army HQ and are here for specific trans-border ops only. So, by the time we gear up, we would appreciate if you could get us those orders from MO.'

It is part truth and part bullshit, but no direct refusal to obey orders, just a gentle reminder to the brigadier to adhere to the chain of command. It was a brilliant excuse—a coup de grâce to our team's further involvement, as getting written orders in the middle of the night from Delhi was next to impossible. The brigadier's face fell as he realised he had just lost half his force.

'Well,' he said turning to the other team commander, 'you better get your boys ready.'

The major was one of those straight-talking simple soldiers known to be sparse with words, other than not having had the privilege of attending the Staff College, where perhaps they taught you the art of disagreeing with seniors. His terse reply was:

'Sorry, sir. The boys are too tired.'

Briefly an incredulous expression glazed across the brigadier's countenance, as if he were unsure of his hearing.

'Are you refusing direct orders, major?' he asked, restraining himself and hoping he had misunderstood. The major nodded his head and repeated himself verbatim. There was no holding him back then, as the brigadier flew into a fury I have rarely seen.

'Insubordination, deputy, that is what it is. You heard him, refusing operational orders from a senior officer. Note the charge. There will be court-martial proceedings. How dare you refuse me! A bloody major refusing to obey orders from a brigadier in a combat zone. I have 25 years of hard service, no hang on, 29, if I add 4 years of NDA, and you have the gumption to say you are tired, when people are dead. Consider yourself attached till further orders.'

And of course, the brigadier carried out his threat and the formation launched a COI (court of inquiry) later. Needless to say, the severe ramifications of wrong verbalisation in the army cannot be compared to a corporate or a civil environment; the repercussions, however, can be equally devastating.

In another incident, I had the privilege to be privy to a very high-profile briefing. As an event, it was a complete antithesis to the above examples and a great personal learning in the subtle art of dissent. The incident taught me that how you dissent is often more important than the dissent itself. The scene was played out at the highest levels of the army, in a room charged with rank, tension and unspoken hierarchies.

In the early 1990s, I was the ADC security to an army chief, or rather, the head of his protection—a glorified title which, in plain Delhi Police speak, translates to 'gunman'. The chief had just taken over command and was a problem-solver with a list of issues he wanted resolved within the period of his command. His first official excursion was to Kashmir, where militancy was at its peak and whose state government of that time was unable to understand the severity of the situation and the response it merited. The town of Sopore had been taken over by hordes of militants and it was a no-entry zone for anyone in uniform. Declaring it a piece of Pakistan, the *jehadis* would fire at army convoys and freely move around, showing their dominance.

Clearly, the army disapproved of the situation, since it was nothing short of waving a red flag to a bull. A Guards battalion came to be deployed in the vicinity, with the aim of cleaning the town, as and when the orders were given from higher HQ. However, those orders never came, as the authority was superseded by the Home Ministry for political reasons. The delay emboldened the militants and the rancour at the other end grew worse between the army and the civil administration or the governor. There was bad blood between the governor and the corps commander—a future chief—and the overall army rank and file on the ground, as they were convinced they were being asked to fight with their hands tied. Into this maelstrom of enmity, the new chief flew in to smoothen ruffled feathers, including of his own senior commanders who felt let down by the Army HQ.

A briefing was arranged at the brigade HQ at Baramulla. The entire top brass of the Northern Army was present, along with the army commander and the DGMO (director general of military operations). As a lowly captain, I found myself an obscure corner from where I could keep an eye on my ward, the chief. Intermittent firing could be heard in the distance, as the brigade commander sought permission from the chief to begin his briefing. He had barely continued for 10 minutes when the chief interjected:

'Tell me, brigadier, if these militants are crossing over from Pakistan using ridge lines and ravines, why have we not used gunships? Surely, they can be engaged in the more uninhabited higher reaches.' The flummoxed brigadier, over-ranked by all the brass, caught the eye of his immediate senior, the divisional commander, who turned to the corps commander and the silent exchange of glances went up the hierarchy, till the army commander spoke up.

'Sir, ideally one should not use gunships in their own backyard, other than the fact that if you do, be sure the Pakis will push in

Stinger missiles. Things will escalate. But if you think it will help,' he continued, in a tone that you take to an uninformed man, 'we can take it up with the Air Force. But before that, we would need written orders from your desk.'

A little later the chief butted in again.

'I am told there are militant training camps across the border and some just a few kilometres from the LOC. Why haven't we taken them out?'

'No problem, sir,' the DGMO stepped in, 'the Prime Minister's Office must sanction any trans-border operation. But if you give the green signal, we will gladly do it.'

'Then you have my permission, gentlemen,' retorted the chief.

'Written orders from your office, sir,' the army commander quipped.

The chief was noticeably getting exasperated and belligerent and the brigadier conducting the briefing was standing around bored, fidgeting with the pointer stick, since he was hardly getting a chance to wedge in a word sideways. His briefing clearly had not gone according to the script. It was turning out to be more of a Q&A session.

'Why haven't you cleared Sopore yet?' The Chief shot the question at the brigade commander. 'I am told the militants jeer and mock the troops and you allow it.'

The army commander took a deep breath and with just an

insinuation of condescension in his tone, replied: 'The orders to enter the town must come from the Home Minister. As you know, an infantry battalion is poised for the strike. But if you, as the chief, give us written orders, it will be sorted out in the next 24 hours. However, let me remind you, sir, that this is Kashmir and not Punjab. Twenty innocents killed here will have international ramifications. The press will be scathing in their reportage.'

The chief had practically no experience of service in the valley. He was a cavalry officer and had commanded the western army before taking over as chief. Under him, the army had also taken some credit, along with the Punjab police, for efficiently handling the Khalistan movement. Everybody present was cognisant of the undercurrent and what the two senior generals were trying to do. They were politely educating him on the nuances of operating in Kashmir, both political and military, and trying to temper down his excessive expectation of quick results, by subtlety suggesting that he ought to spend some more time in office before taking the hard calls.

The chief snapped, discerning what was afoot and how the two generals were hindering all his suggestions on grounds of inexperience. Clearly, the briefing was dead.

'Allow me to share a recurring dream,' he said pointedly to the two generals. 'I imagine myself sailing down the Jhelum on a *shikara*, listening to the gentle music of the *santoor*. And I plan to do this before I hang up my uniform, gentlemen.'

'No problem, sir,' the army commander retorted, 'why wait that long. It can be done tomorrow. Instead of a *shikara,* we can arrange an armed barge and sanitise both sides of the river. However, instead of the gentle music of the *santoor,* I am afraid you might hear the chatter of the machine guns.'

That briefing stands in my humble experience as a perfect example of how to agree to disagree. A resolute chief with a forceful personality and a head full of ideas to resolve the Kashmir quandary went back with an inconclusive outcome. The two senior generals relented to not one of his points, howsoever fatuous they were for the time and the context, without once saying a direct 'no' or 'cannot be done, sir'. And I use the word fatuous for the time and context, because eventually, except for the use of gunships, his other two issues were addressed. In due course of time, Sopore was sanitised and the hitting of militant camps across the line of control became a standard practice.

A corporate example that mirrors this kind of situational awareness, as shown in the above anecdote by the two generals, comes from Apple in the early 2000s, when Steve Jobs—famous for his vision—was pushing for the original iPhone to have no physical keyboard at all, a radical departure from the BlackBerry-dominated landscape.

Some of the senior engineers, including those working on the iPod and Mac touch interfaces, disagreed with Jobs privately. They believed that without a physical keyboard, users might struggle with accuracy, especially business users accustomed to tactile feedback. But instead of confronting him outright, they channelled their disagreement into prototypes—testing multiple interface concepts quietly and iteratively, often outside of official briefings.

One lead engineer reportedly said, 'We did not tell him he was wrong. We just kept showing him better alternatives until he chose the right one himself.'

In other words, it is important in certain situations to

- Understand the gravity of the leader's authority;
- Sense the emotional temperature of the room;
- Sometimes disagree in action rather than declaration; or
- Buy time until the idea is either tested or times itself out.

Much like the army commander's armed barge remark, it was not about saying 'no' outright—it was about reframing the reality in a way the leader could hear, even if he did not agree in the moment. And just like in the Kashmir example, some of those 'fatuous' ideas may become brilliant later—once the timing and context are correct.

Great leaders encourage positive feedback from the rank and file, but then such secure leaders are very rare. They naturally understand the interrelationship between rank and ego, where the higher you rise, the more your ego burgeons—often requiring a conscious effort to keep the two separate.

It is the leader's responsibility to create an atmosphere where juniors feel comfortable to express themselves, without the fear of being ridiculed or berated if in disagreement with the superior. The parallels in the corporate world were striking, where the absence of a safe space to disagree often doomed the juniors, despite the best resources and talent. In my time, I worked with two large private companies, but let me describe my experience at one of them, a bank. Here, the owner/founder led all business discussions and the entire senior leadership would sit mute, nodding their heads in agreement, since experience had taught them that the big boss did not appreciate suggestions, especially if they were contrary to what he was proposing. It clearly came from an arrogance that originates in wealth, power and a certain degree of success, which often drives a founder to assert undue dominance. The 'I' word, present extensively in his vocabulary, was sickening to hear at times. This naturally led to a breakdown in communication with the team and ruined relationships within the team, since it encouraged sycophancy. The organisation sank in due course of time.

What differentiated SF, in my time, was an intentional effort to remain grounded. A young officer with barely a couple of years of service would get opportunities galore for combat experience. It was a phase of conflict and upheaval in the nation's history, with Sri Lanka, Assam, Kashmir, Siachen and Punjab thrown in turn by turn. The north-east was a perennial problem and had been simmering for years, with potential to erupt suddenly and with extreme violence. Throw in a specialisation course or two and with all the ribbons and decorations, you had a uniform that lit up like a Christmas tree. Clearly, with all the ribbons and combat experience, you were a source of envy and it was only human—with all the silent adulation one received—for you to feel a bit heady. My unit, to counter this tendency of youth with humour and humility, had a Nepali saying in those days, '*Ghamand chae nae. Tarie chae*' (I am not arrogant. I am cocky).

Humility and modesty go hand in glove and are not just personal virtues, but professional assets too. It enables teams to function with trust, openness and shared responsibility—essentials in both business and war—since arrogance hinders personal growth, strains relationships and leads to poor decision-making. In the SF, for any tough situation the officer would defer to the men, especially if some of them had more experience. The bond between officers and men was very tight and the officers expected no privileges when out on a mission. I harp about these qualities to impress upon the importance of creating a conducive environment as a leader that encourages free exchange of views and ideas from bottom up. Arrogance and ego will always be huge impediments towards acceptance of the views of your juniors, or for that matter, towards creating that necessary culture which lends comfort to your juniors to disagree with you.

Other than the professional advantages, one will agree that they are also fine qualities to own as a human. In the SF of the older generation, humility curbed a brashness of speech, a desire to boast, which was so essential from a professional confidentiality point of view. In those days, unlike now, special operations, both covert and overt, were treated as classified; also, as a general rule, special ops should never be ideally talked or written about. This is the reason why the SF are called the *silent professionals.* The live telecast of the anti-hostage operation by the NSG during the Mumbai carnage is an example of the complications that were added by the media to the overall planning and conduct of the operation. Shadow ops must remain in the shadows. Modesty forbids showing off and humility keeps you grounded.

In the end, whether navigating the chaos of a combat situation or the complexities of a business environment, the principles stay the same—clarity of purpose, honesty in execution and the humility to listen, learn and lead. The old SF saying about calling a donkey your father captures, in a rustic way, the essence of mission focus; when a job must be done, it must be done. Period. While it focuses on execution, it also emphasises that success often depends on informed participation rather than blind compliance to orders. It is about knowing when to say no and how to say it, but above all, remaining fiercely committed to getting the job done.

Takeaways

- ***Completion is non-negotiable.*** *Once you have accepted a task—deliver. Your word is your contract. See it through, come what may.*

- ***Plans are only as good as their execution strategy.*** *A vision without a clear, detailed method of implementation is just a wish. Build execution into your planning process from the start.*
- ***Clarity precedes commitment.*** *Before taking on a task, make sure you understand it completely. If it feels overwhelming, break it down. Progress, like all great architecture, is built brick by brick. The Japanese call this Kaizen—the practice of making small, consistent improvements every day.*
- ***Set meaningful goals—professionally and personally.*** *You cannot hit a target you do not aim for. Goals create direction, accountability and momentum.*
- ***Effort must yield value.*** *Know your return on effort (ROE) just as clearly as your return on investment (ROI). Time and energy are finite—spend them wisely, measure them meaningfully.*
- ***Learn the art of respectful dissent.*** *Disagreeing with seniors or superiors is not a sign of disloyalty—it is a mark of courage and clarity. But how you disagree matters. Timing, tone and tact are everything.*
- ***Stay grounded—no matter how high you rise.*** *Humility is strength under control. Modesty earns respect. Never let your ego grow larger than your role, or you will stop growing altogether.*

KNOW YOURSELF AND THE MEN YOU COMMAND

The world is run by people. Learn to understand them well.

It is dusk, and the shadows under the trees are shrinking rapidly as they lose their struggle against the advancing darkness. A pale-yellow bulb hanging on a wire comes alive casting a dull glow on a group of soldiers falling in to hear the evening orders. As a young lieutenant, I stand there waiting for the men to form up and for the team sergeant to give the report. I have spent a year with them and most of it in combat in Sri Lanka. I know them well, having spent the bulk of the time on the island sitting immobile for hours in the bush. Undeniably, there is no better way to bond with men than being thrown into combat together.

Just as I am about to start, the team commander, a major, walks up. He asks me a few random questions to check if I am plugged into team affairs and then suggests I spend a little more time trying to get to know the men I am commanding.

'I know them better than their wives, sir,' I retort defensively, 'well, I certainly have spent more time with them than their better halves,' confident that my time with them in combat has made me understand every nuance of their character.

'Switch off that light,' he instructs. Someone reaches up and pulls the bulb out. Darkness and silence engulf the place. I wait, unsure what the major is up to.

'Number five from the right, second row.'

A voice pipes up from the darkness, '*Haan sahib.*'

The major turns to me, 'Alright, Sapru—name, family, hometown, service details, last leave taken,' so on and so forth. This goes on till he has me all muddled up in front of the men. As a parting shot, he tells me about commanding officers in the unit who could recognise nearly 500 men in the unit, from behind, often by their gait or their voice—a testament to the deep bond forged over the years. This is a valuable lesson indeed and a reminder that it is just not enough to know the soldiers by their name, family and background, but also highlighting a crucial lesson: leadership is not about popularity, it is about a genuine connection and respect. The former gets you no respect and begets a retinue of fawning, servile subordinates, who shroud their mediocrity at best, in the garb of pandering to your weakness for acceptance as a leader. Know when to draw the line with your juniors and likewise keep that respectable distance with your boss, unless he allows familiarity, which organically comes about because of mutual professional appreciation.

This lesson transcends the SF into civilian life too—as a leader, understanding your team down to the smallest detail makes the difference between a harmonious efficient unit and a disjointed sycophantic team. In professional lives, it is equally important to establish a balance, gaining the right level of personal rapport with subordinates while keeping a respectful distance from our superiors. In civvy street, I would often tell a newcomer joining my department that ours was first a professional relationship and was based on his professional competence at his job. If he passed that test, I would allow the person into my personal space. Some went on to become lifelong friends, while others remained professional acquaintances. Regardless of the level of competence, every subordinate should always be treated with the same level of respect as one would expect from their own superiors.

It is in the nature of military service—where the price of failure or success, for that matter, is measured in human life—that it needs a much deeper and personal understanding of your subordinates. Considering that the men we commanded hailed from the hinterland of this country, with diverse cultural, religious and linguistic backgrounds, it was imperative that the personal association between the leader and the led had to be very strong, or else he was not going to follow you to hell and back. Every profession, likewise, stipulates the degree of familiarity one needs to ideally have with the team in order to create the most conducive, productive environment. This degree of familiarity also makes it easier for you as a leader to judge the men under your command better, thus giving you the advantage of using them better in a more prudent and productive manner.

For instance, a British brigadier studied men during the Falklands war and slotted them into four categories. *Bottom Failures*—a small number, who were the malingerers, shirkers, cowards, etc. *Survivors*—a vast majority, who did what they were told to do. *Stickers*—utterly reliable, good, solid officers and men. And the last category he calls the *Thrivers*—a small minority of men who cherish the challenges of war and tend to excel. This resonated with the ancient philosophy of Heraclitus, a philosopher in ancient Greece, who expressed it differently. He said that out of 100 men, 10 should not be there; 80 are just targets; nine are real fighters, for they make the battle; and one is a warrior and he will bring the others back. My observation while leading men in combat or on any risky venture led me to slot men in the same four categories. A rare breed which felt no fear or had a remarkably high threshold for risk—Satish, my lead scout in Sri Lanka, comes to mind. While others would recommend caution in a high-risk situation, he alone would sidle up to me and urge instant action. His black eyes would sparkle in anticipation of action, for he clearly loved a good scrap.

The second lot felt fear but did not express it. I would slot myself in that class of men and like to believe that it was the sake of my own reputation and the fear of being labelled yellow that drove me to lead or follow in perilous situations. The third lot felt fear and showed it, but did their job. A cargo load of paratroopers, crammed like sardines in a plane, waiting for the green light to exit, is a perfect body of men to study the subject of fear. Some love it, others are fearful but exhibit complete nonchalance and a third bunch are clearly scared and make no effort to hide their dread. But the moment the light beeps green, to a man they will abandon the aircraft. These men understood what Aristotle said, 'Fear is only morbid when it is out of proportion to the degree of the danger.' The last lot, of course, are the dregs of any fighting unit—men who felt fear, showed it and shirked their duties due to it.

I give the above examples to elucidate the importance of understanding the men under you and slotting them then in a job or a task, according to their skills, reliability, temperament, etc. to get the best out of them. The American SF passionately believe in the adage 'The right man in the right place is a devastating weapon.' This is why most top-tier special operations units conduct a task-specific selection process, unlike most companies which recruit based on qualifications, and in times of growth often hurriedly, to meet the hiring targets. This anomalous situation is often an inadvertent norm in any large organisation, where filling a vacancy expeditiously is more important than finding the right man for the job, which may take time. Often, the army was no different. In my own case, I was temperamentally more inclined to do my combat free-fall course as a specialisation; however, as there were no vacancies that year, I got slotted for the combat diving course or what is, in our jargon, called the Frogmen's course. Perhaps I would have been a better skydiver than the military diver I turned out to be.

A couple of bygone incidents come to mind, which bring out the importance of knowing your men and the loss to the organisation of not employing them in a correct and productive manner:

It was one of those tranquil, balmy Sri Lankan evenings. Having cleared my probation, I had finally been handed over command of my troop for ops. Sitting outside the tent, I asked my buddy to fetch the team barber for a much-needed haircut. The man briefly hesitated and then, as if feeling compelled to act contrary to his wish, went across to the men's quarters. Shortly, a nondescript smiling young man with a noticeable paunch presented himself. His name was Sajjan MT and he hailed from Kerala. From a worn-out satchel he produced the bare minimum tools of his trade. All except for the comb, I noticed, were rusted. The way he handled them before starting, I could guess why they were in that state.

He was struggling with the scissors and trying to figure out how the zero-machine worked. Chatting incessantly in his Mallu Hindi, in the next twenty minutes, he gave me the worst haircut I have ever got. Briefly, the thought crossed my mind that the men were playing a joke with the new officer by sending someone who was not from the trade. There were cuts and lacerations on my scalp, and at one stage, I told him to let it be. The Tamil Tigers, after all, were not really keen on appreciating your hairstyle before taking a pot shot at you, and it did not matter one bit if you went to your maker wearing a crew cut or with an Amitabh Bachchan hair style.

Come evening, I saw him at the volleyball court playing well and with more enthusiasm for the game than the average soldier on the dusty court. Later, as the men lined up before stepping out for an operation, I noticed Sajjan standing sheepishly last in the column, toying with his AK and trying his best to look sufficiently soldierly. Having once suffered at his hands, I was more scared of him than the Tamil Tigers. With personal experience of how he handled the tools of his craft, I was eyeing the weapon in his hand with trepidation. Not sure what to do, I exchanged a furtive look with the senior JCO, who very innocuously nodded his consent. A barber going out with a fighting patrol—not something I had been taught at the military academy.

The moment the JCO had my ok, he looked at Sajjan, who promptly broke ranks and confidently walked right up and took over as the number one scout. Clearly, this was a well-established practice and order of march, since no one showed any surprise. Thereafter, for my entire stay in Sri Lanka, the only two men ahead of me most of the time, when out on a patrol, were Sajjan MT and Satish; both were from Kerala and both could speak and understand Tamil. At the proper time, I got the story from Sajjan and the other men. He wanted to join as a fighting soldier, but there was no vacancy that year. So, he opted and joined as a tradesman and later volunteered for the SF. While the men in the team had tremendous respect for him, none of course ever went to him for a haircut. And though we got the best out of him in ops during our stay in Sri Lanka, it is a pity the army got it all wrong when they hired a fine soldier as a barber.

The other occasion I remember of talent wasted—by putting the wrong man in the wrong job—was in the unit back at the base.

One morning, as the breakfast was getting delayed, I went across in a huff to admonish the cook. Imagine my surprise, as I entered his tiny room next to the kitchen, to discover the entire wall pasted with charts. On closer inspection, I discovered that he had painstakingly drawn organisational charts of various Special Force units from across the world. There was a complete organisational structure of the Pakistani SSG, another of the SAS, and so on. Forgetting what I had come for, I recall getting into an interesting discussion on the subject with him. What a waste, for he would have made a fine SF intelligence operative. Needless to say, his cooking was atrocious. I guess this inclination to be frivolous in not selecting the right resource for the right job is linked to the availability of staff. The bigger the workforce, the lesser is an attempt made to do a thorough screening and assessment of an individual's capability for a particular role—the reason the SF believe in quality over quantity. It was no different in the civilian world.

There were occasions when I took over a department in a new company to discover a few of those unproductive old-timers, well-ensconced in a comfortable job, who had grown in the organisation with the current MD or someone senior in the management. Most had delivered when the organisation was nascent, but over time had stagnated, surviving under the protection of someone at the top. They knew they could not be sacked and were a nuisance. Some of them, who had a shard of self-respect still intact, just about managed their job. One could live with them. But a more dangerous man was the one who was apathetic, occupied a prominent position and had ineptitude that was a threat to the company. Every piece of work would be either stalled, delayed or tawdry, with detrimental repercussions in the future. His presence was also highly demotivating for the rest of the team, who saw lack of effort being rewarded. My attempt in such circumstances was to neutralise the man's corrupting influence by isolating him from the team and ideally giving him an inconsequential job, which would have the minimum damaging effect overall. Such instances reinforced my belief that every workplace thrives best when individuals are evaluated on clear, merit-based criteria and employed as per their strengths. However, the choice of the right man for a particular job is often a challenge, especially in the corporate world.

In the absence of a structured recruitment process, it is difficult to judge a person from first appearances, especially when the person is prepared to present his best image. The carefully manicured façade can often be misleading and character fault lines appear the moment the individual feels he is comfortably ensconced in his job. So, what should one look for when hiring? I would often gauge for common sense—strangely not so common; straight talk; someone who did not hesitate in accepting he did not know the answer; brevity in speech; and clarity in thought. In fact, I was always more impressed with someone who presented a CV which was just a page or two long at a maximum, rather than a mini booklet of exaggerated accomplishments. As a team player, I had a huge bias for those who had played sports, the advantages of which are obvious and need no enumeration here. Another important trait is confidence, which should not be confused with overconfidence, since while the former is always appreciated, the latter quality is a complete put-off in any age, especially in a young person. Such a person is never going to be an easy learner with his overconfident know-all attitude.

Personally, my own approach has always been guided by a keen self-awareness, a principle echoed in the old Sufi adage, 'The only thing I know is that I know nothing and I am not quite sure that I know that.' Strangely, if you constantly remind yourself that it is too big a world out there to know everything, you will invariably develop a mind for inquiry and a willingness to learn. If you have a curious mind that seeks answers, you tend to talk less and listen and ask more. We will discuss the necessity of being a lifelong seeker in more detail further down in the book.

In the old Indian Army, they had an unwritten rule for a young lieutenant just commissioned into his unit. They believed a lieutenant should be seen, not heard. In other words, he should be outdoors spending all his time with the men, listening to them, seeing all and learning constantly. This was followed informally to integrate as quickly as possible the new leader with the led. Having played games on the field, trained and spent time together, informally and formally, the men knew the calibre of the new officer and vice versa; the officer made his own assessment of the character of the men he would command. It also developed mutual respect and naturally fostered constant feedback. In the SF, often as a part of selection, the probationer would have to live with the men in the barracks. Feedback on the officer was always taken from the men at the end of the probation period. I have seen a fine officer who came on probation to us failed on the negative feedback we received about his conduct from the men. This rigorous and informal evaluation process sharpens both the leader and his team and is a practice sorely lacking in the civilian sector (though an ineffectual system of 360-degree appraisal is followed in some of the companies). Other than getting to know each other, it would also stand the young officer in good stead as he grew in service, since by the time he commanded his unit, some of these men would be JCOs and one of them the senior-most trusted aide, the subedar major (SM).

I digress a little, but it would be amiss on my part if I did not narrate an incident highlighting the enormous man-management benefits that accrue from the above practice.

In an operation in Sri Lanka, the Tamil Tigers managed to ambush an entire company plus the strength of an infantry battalion. The CO was wounded, and with a few men, found himself fighting it out isolated from the bulk of his men, as the Tigers managed to break the column with their accurate and heavy fire. Command and control were lost as the column disintegrated, turning the fight individualistic in penny pockets. At some stage during the fighting, the CO gave the unwounded men with him a chance to make a break and get away. The SM refused, saying that he had grown up in the unit with the CO and would prefer now to die with him. I guess that is the ultimate test of leadership when men are prepared to die willingly for you and it speaks volumes for the SM's loyalty and courage as well. Whatever may have been the folly in planning and the misconduct in its execution, clearly courage was not wanting in some quarters. Neither of them made it back, unfortunately. This commitment to duty, underpinned by a sense of shared purpose, is far more potent than any cultivated promise of loyalty often seen in the corporate environment.

Moreover, the existence of a formal recruitment process to join the defence services, with a gamut of tests, which include mental, psychological and physical tests, followed by a medical test, is in stark contrast to the often-informal methods of corporate hiring. In the corporate hiring scenario, more often than not, depending on the position, a few interviews with various seniors in the organisation suffice. When assessing a candidate in such an informal selection method, it becomes imperative to quickly form as exact a reading of the person as possible. I sought out individuals for some of the essential qualities that are necessary for the job in hand and other common values that you interpret from the candidates' overall conduct and personality.

Most of us in our daily lives must quickly gauge and weigh up a person—to trust or not and how much. That trust will then decide how you further conduct yourself with the person. In a not-so-recent past, when arranged marriages were the order of the day, the general belief followed in some quarters when choosing a suitable man for your daughter was to check him out informally for a couple of things, in addition to the usual more visible indicators, i.e., financial status, lineage, etc. You watched for the man's love for animals, especially dogs; his conduct with people below his station—servants and waiters, for example; and his affection for children. To that, I add a love for sports and outdoor activities. Often, if he had the latter attributes, the person was intrinsically a good man. I give this snippet of information to bring forth the point of being aware, when hiring, of some of the basic qualities that you think are essential to evaluate the individual accordingly.

To an ex-soldier, loyalty was an important character trait; but I was inclined more towards organisational rather than personal loyalty. In some of the private firms I worked for, this was often a cause of disagreement, with the owner or founder of the firm expecting a dog-like loyalty to himself, not understanding that if I was loyal to the firm, I was indirectly loyal to him. In the corporate world, while there was an expectation from the employee to be loyal, it was often taken for granted and assumed that it could always be bought at a certain price. Retention of staff was often confused with loyalty. The former can most of the time be bought with money, a higher bonus, salary hike, etc., while the latter is a very personal quality trait and needs a higher moral reason than mere avarice. Companies agonise over the question of employee loyalty to the firm. Most soldiers who quit the army and transitioned to civilian jobs have at some stage or the other been asked this question by the HR department on how one could implant the same degree of loyalty that exists in the army. The answer is you cannot. Let me explain.

The first difference is that the army does not allow entry at various levels. Everybody joins at more or less the same age and at the same level and grinds through the same basic training at a common military academy or training centre. The aim thereafter is to purge the recruit's civilian identity and supplant the civilian value system with that of the military, i.e., from a collective perspective. Darren Moore, in his book on soldiering, mentions that 'basic training is designed to be physically exhausting. Sociologists have empirically confirmed that a severe initiation results in entrants placing a high value on group membership, whereas a mild initiation does not engender the same intensity of commitment to the group. The intensity of basic training therefore, has a correlation with the desired intensity of organisational loyalty.' A guide for officers in the US Air Force mentions a comment: 'It will be seen that it is not primarily a cause which makes men loyal to each other, but rather the loyalty of men to each other which makes a cause.' Amongst the Israeli soldiers, this comradeship is called *achavatt lochameem* (combatants' brotherhood).

This concept of 'achavatt lochameem,' or the combatants' brotherhood, is what got a lot of our men and officers killed in the SF. Captain Davinder Singh Jass (Kirti Chakra) from my unit, as mentioned earlier, certainly went to his grave early trying to protect his buddy, as did a few other fine men in another operation in which Major Mohit Sharma was killed. The lead scout was shot and then a few more suffered the same fate when they tried to pull him back. Perhaps the seasoned Paki *mujahid* was also acquainted with the concept and knew that quality fighting men bind together in times of crisis, each bound by a commitment that goes beyond contractual duty and where one never abandons a wounded or dead comrade. So he sat patiently and picked off with precision shots anyone who attempted to reach the body.

A very essential quality that I would try and gauge when hiring in the corporate world was a person's passion for their craft. Without a proper selection process, it can only be gauged and will remain in the realms of speculation till such time as he is not tested on the job. The passionate drive to test one's skills in life-threatening conditions is going to be absent in the corporate world, where success is measured by routine targets. True passion, a quality so palpable in elite military units, is still a rarity amongst business leaders, whose daily grind lacks the adrenaline and urgency of a battlefield. Pure soldiering is a young man's profession, and unlike in civilian jobs, a soldier is only training in peace throughout the year for that occasional war that may happen once in his service if he is lucky. This training is even more severe in elite units, and like professional athletes, they strive to be better than their adversaries. For most soldiers then, war presents an opportunity to test their skills. During the American-led invasion of Iraq in 2003, the Commanding General David Petraeus was asked by a reporter how he would feel if Saddam backed down. His response was: 'There would be relief at not putting these wonderful soldiers in harm's way. There also might be a bit of a let-down and it would only be that. This is the biggest prize fight in our careers and every soldier at every level has been training for this for months, if not years.'

This passion to test yourself out was somehow not that ubiquitous in the corporate world. That is not to say that it is bereft of good people who are not passionate about what they do. Large business enterprises are not created by 'un-passionate' people who just turn up in office to make a living. But they are rare. Delivery had become routine and there was never any excitement at having a go at the intended target. This is unlike the SF, where you could discern a palpable buzz before any operation, and mind you, this kind of excitement was for a job that could get you killed or maimed. I guess that is the difference in following your passion as a profession, vis-à-vis following a profession as a job.

Integrity, too, follows a binary path in the military and is of course a given in any profession; there are no degrees to it. You are either 100 per cent honest or not, for anything less is an outcome of a lack of opportunity, rather than a considered moral decision, and given the chance, one will eventually succumb to the temptation. We will have more on integrity in a later chapter. General Colin Powell has the following to say on hiring, 'Organization doesn't really accomplish anything. Plans don't accomplish anything either. Theories of management don't matter much. Endeavours succeed or fail because of the people involved. Only by attracting the best people will you accomplish great deeds.'

While the title of the chapter starts with 'Know Yourself', I am covering it at the end of the chapter. As a correlation, it is equally important—while you are striving to go up the professional ladder—to be conscious of your standing within your peer group, seniors and most importantly, your boss. The attempt should be to always ensure that you are amongst the *Thrivers* or as Heraclitus says in the minority 10 per cent and never marked out as one of the *Survivors*. One of the reasons for conducting an unsparing probation in the SF was not only for the organisation to test your limits, but equally for the individual to discover their potential and limits. Not only the SF selection process, but also the overall experience of undergoing military training during your academy days, along with various courses throughout your service career and your annual confidential report in any appointment, gives individuals regular feedback on their strengths and shortcomings. This entire process is absent in the corporate career, where I have often seen bosses hesitant or shying away from giving an honest, blunt appraisal to an individual. This is a great disservice a leader can do to their juniors. My recommendation to those in civilian jobs is to conduct a very brutal honest introspection, ideally as early in life as possible, with feedback from friends, family and your professional peer group—a SWOT analysis of sorts of your strengths and weaknesses, with corrective action. This is not an easy ask, especially when one is burdened with the arrogance and confidence of youth.

Seneca has the following to say on introspection, 'To the best of your ability, demonstrate your own guilt, conduct inquiries of your own into all the evidence against yourself. Play the part first of a prosecutor, then of a judge and finally of a pleader in mitigation. Be hard on yourself at times.'

One of the benefits of this self-analysis is that it will make you aware of the value you bring to the table and its overall impact on the team and the task in question. The nature of the job in SF needed highly skilled small team operations. You were trained to fight at a basic level with a buddy. You covered each other's back, fought as a buddy pair and stood by each other through thick and thin unto death if the occasion so demanded. The training then progressed to fight in larger numbers, i.e., squads of 5–6 men, then to a troop of around 4 squads, and so on. When you fight in such small numbers, it is imperative that each man is highly trained in primary and secondary skills to complement each other and enhance the overall fighting efficacy of the team.

For example, a squad, which is the smallest fighting unit, could have a specialist medic, a sniper, a demolition expert and so on and so forth, depending on the op, with every member having rudimentary knowledge of each other's skill set. Each man brought some value to the team. The inference I draw from this is simply that every individual, at every stage of life, has a responsibility to contribute positively to the group they belong to—be it a team, a family, an organisation or a nation.

This sense of contribution is not something that magically appears in a job. It begins early. Think of a school project team—there is always that one student who organises the slides, another who does the research and still another who rehearses the presentation. When each person plays their part, the outcome is effortless and excellent. That is value addition. No one has a role that is glamorous—but each role is vital. That is teamwork without titles.

In high-stakes environments—combat, corporations or a crisis—the group only moves forward when every individual shows up and contributes their unique value—not occasionally, not when convenient or only in a crisis, but as a way of life.

Value is not just about performance metrics or salary brackets. It is about ownership, initiative and the quiet commitment to make things better wherever you are.

This overarching mindset of always trying to add value in whatever you try is justifiably one of the most significant reasons why certain organisations and companies flourish, and as a corollary, societies and countries benefit too. This can only come about if one is open to introspection, with a view to estimate candidly one's contribution at a basic level, from childhood onwards through one's professional as well as personal journey. 'Human improvement,' as Froude said, 'is from within outward.'

The Buddhist Japanese monk Nichiren Daishonin bolsters the importance of the above and mentions that 'ideally it should all begin with the individual taking responsibility for his own life, by reforming themselves first. Followed with ameliorating the immediate environment and relations and then extending their own knowledge, compassion and the overall life into a wider world.'

In closing, whether you stand on a battlefield or in a boardroom, understanding yourself, your boss and the people you command is the cornerstone to achieving success. Missions are accomplished when you know exactly what you expect from yourself and those around you. The key to any high-performing environment—military or corporate—is a culture rooted in purpose, trust and shared goals. The military achieves this through structure, discipline and a deep sense of belonging. While the corporate world may face challenges in replicating this depth of connection, it can, however, still cultivate it—through clear values, honest feedback and a commitment to continuous self-reflection.

True progress begins when individuals—not systems—take ownership. When we hold ourselves to higher standards, when we align our personal growth with the collective mission, we build better organisations and better people. Token appraisal processes often struggle to replicate the deep level of connection so necessary to achieve goals.

Takeaways

- ***Know your people—deeply and intentionally.*** *In leadership, familiarity is not a given—it is a mission-critical advantage. Whether leading soldiers or teams, trust is built when you take the time to understand strengths, weaknesses, motivations and fears.*
- ***Choose respect over popularity.*** *Do not chase cheap applause or overfamiliarity. Let professional relationships grow on the foundation of competence, fairness and consistent performance. Popularity fades; credibility endures.*
- ***Stay conscious of where you stand.*** *Always know your performance bandwidth amongst peers—not for ego, but for self-regulation. Strive to stay amongst the top performers, not to compete with others, but to compete with your potential.*
- ***Hire for character, not just credentials.*** *Be a sharp judge of people. The right person in the right role can transform outcomes. Look beyond résumés—observe temperament, adaptability and integrity.*
- ***Practice brutal introspection.*** *Growth demands honest self-appraisal. Periodically step back and ask: am I still*

learning? Am I still aligned with what I stand for? No tool sharpens the self like self-awareness.

- ***Define the traits you want around you.*** *Whether hiring, mentoring or assembling a team—look for reliability, initiative, humility and resilience. These are the qualities that sustain performance when the pressure peaks.*
- ***Embrace the concentric circle of responsibility.*** *Start with the self, then expand outwards—to team, to organisation, to society. Your value lies not just in what you do, but in how far your actions positively ripple.*
- ***Recognise the military edge.*** *Soldiers—especially in SF—carry a mindset honed in adversity: clarity, grit, accountability and deep team orientation. These traits are prized far beyond the battlefield—and applicable in any high-stakes profession.*
- ***Infuse your work with passion and purpose.*** *As the Japanese concept of Ikigai suggests, fulfilment comes from the intersection of what you love, what you are good at, what the world needs and what you can be paid for. Find that centre—and show up for it daily.*

RANK DOESN'T MAKE A LEADER

My centre is giving way. My right is retracting. Situation excellent. I am attacking.

–Ferdinand Foch

To know your men is just one part of the spectrum of man management, since without leadership, just understanding your men is not going to get you the required results. Leadership is about guiding, inspiring and sometimes toughening the collective resolve. Much has been written and lectured about leadership, starting from the basic question: are leaders born or made? I guess if it were the former, most military academies for officers across the world would be shutting shop in the absence of finding enough young men who were born leaders to warrant running such large establishments. Leadership is not just about owning any one essential personality trait, but is a complex collection of attributes. While some personal qualities are still common, characteristics will vary in degrees as per the profession in question. The attribute of courage, for example, so necessary for a military leader, may not be necessarily as important for, say, someone in the corporate world. The art of command is intrinsically the art of dealing with human nature. A few anecdotes to elucidate some of those values would be in order.

Field Marshal Sam Manekshaw narrated an incident when he went on a visit to a Pakistani POW camp after the 1971 war. The SM, the senior-most enlisted man, was introduced and he escorted the field marshal around the camp. The field marshal, then the army chief, insisted on being taken to the cook's house, where he tasted the food first and then requested to be shown the men's latrines. Finding the place clean and to his satisfaction, he asked for the sweeper or the *jamadar*, as the term was used in those days. A nervous young man was presented and the field marshal shook his hand, much to the surprise and dismay of the prisoners standing around. It was confounding to see such a big man shake the hands of a lowly sweeper, a tradesman as they are called in the army. At the time of seeing off the field marshal, the SM came to attention and requested permission to speak freely. I paraphrase:

'Now I know, *jenab*,' he said, 'why you won the war. You came as the chief, inquired about our problems, tasted our food, checked the latrines and then complimented and shook hands with the sweeper. Our officers would have never done anything of this sort. They live like nawabs.'

I cite the anecdote as an example of what great leadership is really about. Nobody would have criticised him if he had not paid a visit to any of the many POW camps in the country. He had won the war and had more important things to attend to. And even if he did, it could have been a cursory inspection, just to tick the box. But then he was aware that even though they were soldiers of a vanquished army, they were still officially under his command while they served their prison term in India. Their welfare was therefore his responsibility. The field marshal showed empathy and a humane side to his nature, a quality always appreciated by subordinates, other than what has been mentioned earlier as the Toyota management mantra: *Genchi Genbutsu* (go and see). The devil lies in the detail, and the field marshal made it a point to taste the food and inspect the toilets. Never neglect details—especially as you go up, the teams become larger and you start delegating, the chances of something falling between the cracks exponentially increases.

In the modern leadership jargon, the style of leadership the field marshal exhibited resonates with the concept of a servant leader. Instead of focusing on his own goals, success and power, the leader's primary aim is to serve the juniors or subordinates. Their well-being and development are more important than his personal agenda. Briefly, servant leaders encourage independent action and thought and create a culture of empowerment and strong relationships, where problems are addressed before they become critical. While the army does not necessarily know the modern HR jargon, the training and grooming over the years naturally emphasise these qualities in leaders. In fact, no better example can be given than the 'Chetwode Code,' which forms the motto of the Indian military academy and states:

'The safety, honour and welfare of your country comes first, always and every time. The honour, welfare and comfort of the men you command comes next. Your own ease, comfort and safety comes last, always and every time.'

The field marshal was open to suggestions and asked for honest feedback. They say in the army that the day soldiers stop bringing you their problems is the day you have stopped being their leader. There should always be an easy and honest communication bottom up. The day it stops is the day either your subordinates stop having any confidence in your problem solving or conclude that you do not care. Either way it is a failure of command. I never ever ran into a CEO or MD in my corporate life who would, at random, leave the corner office and just stroll down the aisles chatting up informally with the junior employees in the building. How much he would learn about morale and problems in the rank and file! In the unit, it was routine to regularly interact with all levels of your team. It reassures the members, other than giving you a real-time understanding of the pulse of the men under your command. Seasoned soldiers will tell you that just by driving around the unit area, one can make a fairly correct assessment of the state of affairs in the unit. Do young soldiers on seeing the top brass shy away or come forward to greet? The way they salute, the confidence in the greeting, the tilt of the beret, the swagger, the way they carry their weapon etc.—so many visible indications if a body of men are healthy, happy and fighting fit.

Let me enumerate another quality of leadership with a few personal anecdotes. We are in tents pitched in the middle of a forest somewhere in north Kashmir. It has been snowing heavily for the last couple of days, making sleep quite impossible as the tents keep collapsing throughout the night with the accumulating snow. A burst of gunfire wakes me up. I check the time; it is two in the morning. Grumbling, I step out to check. There is commotion at one of the sentry posts located at the periphery of the forest. Two very agitated and shaken sentries step forward to explain. A pair of leopards, not finding their usual prey, in desperation decided to bag a human—the only easily available food source in the peak of winter.

I shine my torch and make out the distinct pug marks in the snow coming out of the forest and approaching to within ten feet of the bunker. At that stage, one held back and the other leapt. Miscalculating the distance, the big cat landed on the sandbags knocking the LMG barrel. As the man with the weapon fell back with a shout, his number two behind opened up with his AK.

Anyway, come morning and the weather clears up; life big and small, hitherto hunkered for survival, thaw their bodies and shed the lethargy that had gripped everyone because of the inclement weather. The chatter on the militant radios picks up and everyone is asking everyone if they are alright.

Then a familiar commanding voice comes on air. I recognise the voice and know him from his radio call sign as Sher

Khan—a Pakistani and the local Lashkar (LeT) commander for Lolab. He is a calm, cool man and we have often exchanged greetings and spoken on the radio. But today, he is in a foul mood as he berates a Kashmiri militant.

'Where are the rations?' he snaps. 'You promised you would be back in a day or two and now it is five days. How do you think we will survive sitting in this hideout in the forest? We are your guest *mujahid*s and this is how you conduct a *jehad*! And while you are at it, make sure you get a *hakim* (doctor) along. Last night, Javed got mauled by a *sher* (leopard) and is in bad shape.'

My ears pricked up when I heard the last sentence. So, the cats, having missed a meal at our camp, had gone after Javed, who I imagined must have come out to take a leak or was on sentry duty. Either way, it was too tempting for me not to take a gleeful dig at SK. So, I butted into the conversation.

'Sher Khan brother,' I said, 'great, our leopards did finally get you.'

'Oh, come on, *fauji bhai*, leave the channel, I am having a bad day.'

'This is what comes of not coming out to fight,' I said, 'now we have trained these leopards to hunt you all. And do not forget,' I continued, '*Inshah Allah*, if you die mauled by a leopard, you are not going *to jannat* and you can certainly forget the seventy-two virgins.'

I heard a loud chuckle at the other end.

'Hahaha, you make my day, *fauji bhai*,' he retorted. 'Forget the 72 *houris*, brother, in the state I am, present one and I will not be able to do justice to her. All I need now is 72 *chapattis*.'

Both of us had a good laugh. In those miserable conditions, witty banter was therapeutic and the few of us who had been privy to the conversation went about the day feeling much better. After all, it seemed everybody was having a dreadful day in office, including the opposition. People often underestimate the power of humour; when used appropriately, levity can defuse tension in challenging times. This incident, while laced with humour, reveals something fundamental about leadership—sometimes, the ability to stay human, to share a laugh even with your adversary, is what holds the morale of a team together when everything else is collapsing—quite literally.

In another incident, a few days later, the brigade commander visited our post. Someone must have mentioned to him that I often chatted with the militants. Over a beer, he asked me if I could get someone on the radio for a *guftagu* (chat). As a rule, I would only speak with the foreign *mujahids*. I tried a few stations and finally got someone who sounded Punjabi and was willing to talk.

'Brother, *salaam*,' I said, 'all good with you?'

'Barring the weather and the food situation, Allah has been merciful.'

'Hang on,' I said, 'you sound like a local. Any guest *mujahids* around that I can speak with?'

'Yes, yes,' he replied, 'one of them is here.'

'Good, where?'

'In my pyjamas,' the cheeky blighter replied. 'Should I pull them down!'

The brigadier and everyone around burst out laughing. The entire atmosphere lightened and briefly thereafter, forgotten was the stress, impending ops, casualties and the volatile environment we were all existing in.

Before moving to Kashmir, I had been posted in the army headquarter on the staff of the then chief of the army. I was accompanying the chief as his ADC on an inspection tour somewhere in Rajasthan. The corps commander, along with all the senior officers in the formation, was waiting for the chief at the corps HQ. A Sikh Light Infantry guard of honour was detailed to present arms to the chief. It was one of those typical formal army gatherings, all spit and polish, and the whole atmosphere was tense. There was no chitter-chatter, since everybody waited for the chief's arrival in silence.

The guard commander, a tall dark Sikh NCO, went down the lines of his men, running a critical eye over their dress and posture. In the distance came the faint sound of the siren as the chief's cavalcade approached. Suddenly, a peacock alighted in the patch of green in front of the guard of honour and spreading its tail, began dancing. It was a beautiful, calming sight and very soothing to the nerves as everybody quietly watched. The guard commander at that instance looked over his shoulder, and noticing the peacock, dashed at it, throwing stones and using the choicest of Punjabi expletives. The act jarred everyone's sensibilities and the corps commander promptly asked the NCO why he got after the poor peacock. In chaste Punjabi, he answered, '*Sahib*, the chief is arriving and all this sister f....! can think of is dancing on such a serious occasion!' Only the chief's arrival, thereafter, cut short the laughter that ensued.

Humour or levity in any situation is uplifting, in combat it is a force multiplier. The ability to laugh at yourself and at the predicament of the moment can lighten the situation. Humour, when used appropriately and in a timely manner, can create a more conducive work environment, reduce stress, motivate and enhance interpersonal communication. Lord Moran mentions that only humour helped during the First World War: 'Humour that made a mockery of life and scoffed at our own frailty. Humour that touched everything with ridicule and had taken the bite out of the last thing, death.' In my own case, I can confidently say that humour helped me tremendously in sailing through some extremely hard times. My imaginative mind helped me distance myself from the ongoing stress and discomfort of a situation and view the whole thing in a jocular manner. I had some great laughs both in and out of the army.

It is another day at Army HQ and one of the slots in the chief's busy schedule is reserved for a meeting with an ITBP team which is just back from Nepal after having summited Everest. I receive the team and march them into the chief's office. You can notice the pride on each man's face. The chief shakes hands, shares a cup of tea and makes the right utterances for the occasion. The team leader then steps forward and presents the chief with an ice axe. The chief noticeably looks touched, and turning around, instructs me to take down the massive oil painting hanging above the mantelpiece.

'Hang the ice axe there,' he tells me, 'I can look at it from my desk,' he continues, turning to the men, 'and every time I see it, I will remember you brave boys and your achievement.'

An exceptionally fine gesture, I think to myself as I escort the team out of the office. That is how you motivate people. Barely is the last man out when I hear him shout for me.

'Get that ugly axe off, please,' he tells me coldly, 'and put my painting back, will you?'

Now, you can imagine my surprise and disappointment, but although puzzling, this episode underscores the complex interplay between public gestures and private expectations. Anyway, I will get to the learning later; in the meantime, let me first narrate an anecdote from history.

In a war council, where the invasion of Italy is under discussion during the Second World War, Bernard Montgomery is asked which army under his command he would be considering for the landings. One of the officers from his staff pipes up from the sidelines, 'The Eighth Army, of course, General'. And the general apparently turned around with a bewildered look and inquired blankly, 'Which Eighth?'

Now, anybody who has read the African campaign knows Monty, as he was known, defeated Erwin Rommel while he was commanding the Eighth Army in North Africa. His claim to fame was because of the fighting spirit of the Eighth. This may seem like arrogance and ingratitude, clearly. But it is not.

Both anecdotes, while completely dissimilar in setting, bring out the leaders' ability to keep emotions and personal prejudices out of professional decisions. Monty had a job to do in Africa and the Eighth Army was the best equipped to deliver the goods. Having moved on to a new assignment and a new task, his mind had already severed its emotional connection with the Eighth. Often in the army, and more often in the corporate world, I have seen the manager's inability to sack people or a reluctance to appoint the right man for the right job only because it may hurt someone's feelings. Rommel sacked one of his divisional commanders, General Streich, a decorated soldier, for losing a battle and rebuked him gruffly.

'You were far too concerned with the well-being of your troops.'

To that, Streich stiffly saluted and retorted, 'I can imagine no greater words of praise for a division commander.'

Both, in a way, were great leaders. One who would sacrifice

anything for the completion of a task and another who would stand by his men. It is a great example to show how decisions really depend on a person's perspective on the path he would like to go down in a comparable situation. When faced with tough decisions, detach personal sentiments from objective analysis, even though the choices may seem harsh initially.

There is another rare man-management quality that I noticed in a few of the bosses I reported to and I consciously avoid using the word *leadership* here, since I did not really get down to acquiring the trait myself, though I can tell you it is very effective, especially if one has to convey a dressing-down to an individual or a group. It is having the *savoir faire* to switch your persona to suit the occasion. The chief's gesture in the earlier anecdote, where he played a perfect host to the Everest team, while in all probability mentally he was present somewhere else, falls under that realm.

I recall travelling with the army chief on a visit to the north-east. The first port of call was the governor's residence-cum-office in Nagaland. Reports had reached the chief from his corps and division commanders of the governor's constant interference in running their commands. Well, perhaps the governor could not help himself, since after all he had retired as a corps commander of the same formation, before being selected as the governor. In service, he was senior to the chief. Those were the days when the north-east competed with Kashmir in an unabated cycle of violence. The chief had clearly flown in especially to rein in the governor and prevent him from interfering in military affairs.

As the personal bodyguard, I would sit in the front seat and inadvertently be privy to a lot of conversations. The chief was in a good mood during the car ride to the residence, joking all the while with his military assistant (MA), a colonel on his staff. The entire caboodle of the top brass was hanging around to receive the boss. The moment the chief stepped out of the car, his entire deportment and expression went through a change, which even a child could have discerned as a harbinger of ill tidings to follow. He strode belligerently into the private office of the governor and banged the door. A murmur of conversation carried out of the room, then a slight increase in the governor's pitch, which was at once drowned in the loud bellowing by the chief. Clearly, he was having the last word on the subject.

Now it is a credit to the training imparted at the military academy, if I may digress a little, where the unwritten custom followed by juniors in a situation where the seniors were getting berated or punished was to come to attention or join them. Without any order given, I noticed, every officer and soldier present on hearing the shouting match between the two senior-most men had come to attention. This was amazing to think, considering that the corps commander had been out of the academy for three decades. Anyway, the chief stormed out and before getting into the car, met his MA's gaze and gave him a conspiratorial wink. Then, as we drove away, he turned to his MA and asked, chuckling, 'So, how was the show, Col *sahib*?'

'Well played, sir,' replied the colonel, 'should not have any further problems from him.'

In another personal experience, I was the subject and at the receiving end of a similar show of unwarranted belligerent behaviour, where the boss's sole intention was to convey to me and to the senior leadership his overall displeasure. This was at a private bank I worked for, where the MD was also the founder and one of the largest individual equity stakeholders. He was a known bully with a vile, foul tongue, given to hectoring, browbeating and badgering his subordinates. He was, like most people who make it big in life, also a good judge of character. Once, during a senior leaders' conference, the MD was clearly unhappy with my performance and true to his style wanted to pitch into me in his typical abusive way. However, his reading of me possibly cautioned advice, to tread carefully, for I may not be the kind of man who would sit back and take it lightly. So, he picked on my number two instead and gave him a severe dressing down, telling him plainly to put in his papers. It was a simple jack-in-office nastiness act, knowing fully well that the average person is not used to unpleasantness and tends to get intimidated. I, of course, got the message which is exactly how he intended. We disbursed and ten minutes later, the secretary informed me that the boss wanted to see me. That had me a little worried, for I had him pinned down as a perfect school yard bully. Maybe I had read him wrong. There was another gentleman with him as I walked into his office. The MD was all effusive charm and fulsome in his praise for my work as he introduced me. If I had not seen this change of personae in some of my earlier bosses before, this volte-face would have completely knocked me over.

This judicious use of bluff, theatrics and an unpredictable temperament keeps people on their toes. While I never did subscribe to it personally, I mention it here as one of the traits I observed, often misunderstood by the average person. Watching Trump on TV, pitching mercilessly into Zelensky, somehow reminded me of this trait—a first-class display of bluff, theatrics and bullying. The message was clear to not only Zelensky, but I guess, as intended, to the rest of the world leaders who had to deal with him in the future. Develop the emotional intelligence to read your audience. Switch your communication style as required by the context, ensuring that your team stays motivated and clear about expectations. There were, of course, on the other hand, bosses I had who were unsure of their jobs, so they were uncertain of their temper. Half the time, subordinates were only inquiring about the boss's mood before taking any issue up to him and so, important stuff was often lost in transit because the boss, most of the time, preferred to stay in a foul mood.

Having acknowledged the importance of tailoring one's communication style, let me touch upon another common and oft repeated leadership quality, the imperative to simply lead, no matter the circumstances. The principle of direct leadership comes into sharp focus when examined under the lens of real-life scenarios in challenging times. As Simon Sinek states, 'There are only two ways to influence human behaviour: you can manipulate it, or you can inspire it'. Let me stick to inspiring, since manipulation is fraught with dangerous consequences if tried with frontline soldiers, especially during war.

Hafruda forest in Kupwara district in Kashmir is a place the SF in the old days was well acquainted with. For it was their favourite game reserve. Mountainous, deep ravines, thick forest and rocky outcrops made it a perfect place to test your skills, for the odds were matched equally in favour of both the hunter and the hunted. The considerable number of kills the SF has bagged over the years has come with its fair share of both officer and other rank casualties on our side. For the small area Hafruda occupies, the casualty ratio has been inordinately high. One day perhaps, the army will dedicate a memorial at the fringes of the forest to all the young lives we lost there.

Sometime in March of 2009, a fighting patrol from my unit led by the indomitable Major Mohit Sharma clashed with a heavily armed *fidayeen* group. In the ensuing gunfight, we lost eight including Mohit, while the entire group of 12 Pakistani militants was neutralised. Anyway, Mohit was awarded the Ashoka Chakra, posthumously, but this is not about Mohit, since his tale is well-known. It is about the man commanding the unit when the incident happened, Col Vinu Nambiar (now a major general). The colonel was a firm believer in the Sicilian proverb '*lu sangu lava lu sangu*' (blood washes blood), or as the Hindustani proverb goes, 'blood will avenge blood,' and a lot of blood had been spilt on his side, which could now only be assuaged with the blood of the perpetrators. The Indian Army, and the SF in particular, do not take to a beating kindly. The account had to be squared.

The colonel's first order of the day was to personally land up at ground zero and take command. Thereafter, as he said, 'I pulled in my remaining two teams that were operating in different sectors of the valley and instructed the other troops milling around to vacate the area of the incident and give me and my boys a clean playing field. This was now personal between the SF and the *mujahideen*.'

Breaking into smaller bodies, the SF teams infiltrated into the forest and the few villages on the periphery to seek contact or ferret the militants out, forcing them to engage. In the next 36 hours of relentless exertion and discomfort, since it was still cold on the heights, the executors set about extracting a terrible retribution. A couple of militants were shot while fleeing a village, some were caught in the forest and one of them thought that the last place the SF would search would be where the first contact had taken place.

It was a belief amongst soldiers during the First World War that the safest place during shelling was to seek cover in an existing shell crater, following the logic that there was a one-in-a-million chance that another shell would land in exactly the same spot. The Taliban followed the same supposition in Afghanistan when the Americans bombed them from the air.

However, they forgot the world had changed. With precision smart bombs riding lasers, collecting in an existing shell crater was the last thing they should have done. The lone *mujahid* followed the same hypothesis that the last place he would run into any opposition would be where it had all started. Wrong. And the last place you test antiquated theories is up in a forest against an enraged bunch of professional soldiers. He was the last of the dirty dozen that had crossed over the border. The account had been squared.

I recall that there was one of our sister SF units on the island, whose CO would often tag along with any troop or a team going out on ops, asserting all the while that he was there only as an observer. To the anxiety of clashing with a Tiger fighting patrol, the officers and men had the added stress of protecting the CO, other than the trepidation of operating under his constant scrutiny and getting ticked off for some minor mistake or the other. It curbed the style and authority of the man in command. Clearly, the CO's conscience bothered him to send men under his command out in harm's way while he stayed behind in the safe environs of the post. The rest of the officers finally had to request him to desist from this practice.

Years later, I ran into him as a brigade commander up in north Kashmir. I was pleasantly surprised on a misty morning to see soldiers appearing out of the forested hill opposite my post, with the tall form of the brigadier in the vanguard. The surprise was not to see him right in front of the leading column, for he had a reputation for doing that in the regiment, but the fact that he was there. For he was supposed to be commanding his brigade in a peace station somewhere in UP.

'Pure boredom, where I am commanding,' he tells me, as I served him some breakfast. 'Nagged Army HQ to allow me a visit to a combat area. Good for the boys. Made them climb the mountain from the other side at night. It is a bit rough. Did not expect so much undergrowth though.'

When the going gets hard and risky, the teaching of leading from the front by the senior-most in command is ingrained in every officer—the ability to roll up your sleeves and pitch in with the boys. The Kargil War saw a lot of commanding officers right in the front echelons of the assaulting force, and of course, an inordinate number of fatalities amongst the junior leadership who invariably led all assaults. The learning I gained was that the situation and task would decide my presence and involvement and to what degree. The idea is not to follow any of the fancy management fads, or your own temperamental management style, but have the flexibility, like the Chinese say, of a 'good bamboo, that bends with the wind'—the knack of knowing 'when to lead, follow or get out of the way'.

All these accounts not only underscore the courage demanded of a leader on the front lines but also set the stage for understanding the multifaceted nature of leadership, where the ability to switch between styles from transformational to transactional defines success. When the chips are down and a crisis looms, as the commander, step forward and lead.

Modesty forbids, but I am reminded of a small incident which gave me enormous joy and in a small way highlights the impact on men, of setting an example by leading. A few years ago, I had gone back to the unit for our usual reunions on the Raising Day. The JCOs of the unit were lined up to welcome and meet the old officers. As I reached the end of the line, shaking hands and introducing myself, the SM requested me to step aside. Ten JCOs then fell in separately, as the SM told me they wanted to meet me in private. It happened that all of them were recruits when I was posted as a company commander at the Parachute Training Centre.

'Twenty-five of us volunteered for the unit because of you,' the SM told me. 'Ten made it through the selection.'

I recalled handpicking a few of them from my company, including the SM, but the rest were unknown.

'And why would so many of you volunteer for the unit,' I asked, 'especially the ones standing here from the other companies at the training centre, who clearly had no interaction with me personally?'

The unanimous answer was that I was the only company commander who made the effort to run the speed marches with them. Imagine, that is all it took, a couple of 40-kilometre runs to motivate so many to volunteer for the SF.

The above are all examples of leading from the front, or if we were to use HR parlance, a transformational/servant leadership style, where the leader inspires and motivates his team by setting an example. His presence at the front or amidst them motivates people to give their best. This style also fosters a deep loyalty to the leader. The opposite of it is what you often see in the corporate world, a more hands-off transactional leadership. Here, the leader focuses on a noticeably clear give and take with his team. Performance is to be rewarded for meeting expectations and likewise, disciplined for not achieving goals—generally followed for task specific and short-term goals. When department or institutional goals are to be done and team effort has to be harnessed, learn the art of sifting the essential from the inessential. Leadership is the nuanced art of balancing risk and resourcefulness. It is not merely about bold decisions all the time, but also about knowing when to adapt and make do with what is available. The size and nature of the task will dictate what needs to be done personally, what should be dropped completely or postponed for a later stage and what should to be delegated. The situation will also thereby dictate the style of leadership that needs to be adopted, i.e., situational, servant, transformational, etc. other than also deciding the degree of micro or macro management it necessitates.

The Indian Army had a three-tier organisational structure, i.e., three sections to a platoon, three platoons to a company, three companies to a battalion (a HQ company is added at this level), three battalions to a brigade and so on. To avoid any confusion as to when a commander should ideally lead in battle or any crisis, they had an informal expectation, where in any given situation, if two-thirds of the force under the command of a person was committed, he was expected to lead. For example, if two platoons were committed in action, the company commander would ideally lead and so on. Most SF operations are small team actions and the few times I saw the CO tag along with us in Sri Lanka was when two of the assault teams were committed for a tasking.

Other than leading from the front, the other leadership quality shown by the CO in the earlier Mohit Sharma anecdote was the determination to finish the task no matter what happens—a consequence clearly of his SF grounding. A job is not done till it is done. He could have easily called off the operation after he had accounted for half a dozen militants. That is not a bad haul and going after the remaining cornered, highly trained militants, in bad terrain and visibility could have easily bought him more casualties. As the CO, his neck was on the block. And I mention this in passing only because, often in my corporate experience, when I gave someone a job to do, I noticed this gap between my expectation of a finished task and the person's understanding of what constituted closure to the job. For example, on inquiring if the job was complete, the answer would be a confident 'Yes, boss. I shot off the mail.'

'And.'

'Well, he has not responded yet.'

'I don't care,' would be my standard reply. 'There was a time limit, you accepted the job, now go to his office or his home, wherever. Finish the bloody job.'

The average corporate mail traffic is congested with what I call the 'corporate mail ping-pong.' The mail exchanges will continue back and forth with naught to show in productivity or the closure of the job. The cover-your-arse syndrome emanating from the senior-most boss sets the culture in a company or department. Work expands to fill up time and execution becomes the casualty. 'The merit of any action lies in finishing it to the end,' I believe Genghis Khan said this to his sons.

Ram Charan states: 'The intellectual challenge of execution is in getting to the heart of the issue through persistent and constructive probing.' While the army understands this concept and builds it into its plans, the corporate world often misses this point. Execution in business is not merely about implementing plans; it is about addressing the core challenges that impede success. Charan emphasises that the true test lies in identifying and understanding the root causes of issues, rather than just their symptoms. This requires a mindset of persistent inquiry and constructive dialogue.

In the army, you are taught that during an attack, once the objective is taken, which is the aim, immediately go forward, dig in and prepare yourself for the enemy's counterattack, an aim plus. A job must be done in totality and if you can throw in a bit of initiative and deliver more than what was asked for, well then as Rudyard Kipling says, 'If you can fill the unforgiving minute, with sixty seconds' worth of distance run, yours is the earth and everything that's in it.'

Let me narrate another account, not a classical example of audacious leadership which involves leading men from the front into the jaws of death. None can deny the sheer courage it takes to be right in front when the lead is flying, exhorting your men to follow you to their deaths. And in our recent national memory, we saw that happening in the Kargil War, where young officers, defying the terrain constraints, led attacks onto hitherto insurmountable peaks. At its basic, it was WWI tactics at high altitude and at an excessive cost in lives. But my next anecdote, while bringing out in abundance qualities of transformational leadership, i.e., leading from the front, also brings out another side of a leader—competence. The year is 1999 and the Kargil War is reaching its zenith, as the Indians go on the offensive. Let me now narrate it in the words of then Major Gurpreet Singh, now a serving major general.

'I was posted as an Instructor at the Artillery school when the Kargil War got underway. Sometime around the end of May, a signal arrived directing me to report forthwith to Muntodhaloe. On reporting, I was told to be the anchor OP (observation post) responsible for arty fire support, for a simultaneous seven-column attack on three features, Point 5300, Ring Contour and Tekri, across a frontage of nearly 3 kilometres. Within 48 hours, from a peaceful classroom, I was thrust into the fray and found myself breathlessly climbing up to my vantage point at around 15000 feet. Talk about acclimatisation!

'The attacking force included men from three units—a Gurkha and a Para battalion, along with a team from the SF. The attack began at night as the men started scaling the heights and by morning, Point 5300 had been captured, sustaining light losses due to mines and machine gun fire. A party of a dozen-plus men had managed to get a toehold on the treacherous summit. At this stage, the officer in command noticed a large body of Pakistanis forming up for a counterattack and requested immediate close fire support. Now, close would be an understatement, for the safety distance when engaging with Bofors is around 300 metres, while the Pakis were at 100 metres and closing the distance fast. Sir, you can imagine my quandary. What enemy! You were being asked to shell your own men. What in military jargon is called, blue on blue. I asked the officer to repeat his request. Affirmative, came a desperate and despondent reply.

I had a hundred guns at my call, waiting impatiently, a dozen or so kilometres down in the valley. I gave a couple of ranging shots and then let loose with a barrage, telling our boys to seek whatever shelter they could under the rocks. The attack was aborted since the Pakis scattered for cover and later retreated. A search of the area revealed 33 enemy bodies. For all the political controversy the guns had created when they were bought, they were now paying back with interest. In the meanwhile, other fire requests were coming in from the attacks in progress on the Tekri and the Ring Contour. An enemy machine gun engaging from a well-concealed *sangar* (stone/rock shelter) was spewing destruction on the vulnerable troops climbing in the open. The officer leading the assault requested pinpoint shelling on the *sangar.*

Imagine jagged peaks, close proximity of your own troops, constantly changing weather conditions, high altitude terrain and all the fog and confusion of a battle and you have a nightmarish situation for taking a shoot. And it occurred to me, how perfect a scenario it was for things to go wrong. All it needed was one shell to go astray and I would have blood on my hands. I asked for a one-gun shoot and can you believe my luck sir, the first round blew the *sangar* to smithereens. It seemed 'Wahe Guru' was perched on my shoulder all the while taking the shoot, for no gunnery school had prepared me for such a scenario. I was making up my own fire support rules and decided on a 1000 rounds minimum on each objective before the attack went in, vis-à-vis the 250-300 rounds recommended as per the manuals to soften a target. Further counter attacks came in on Point 5300 later at night and by the third day the Pakis figured out my position and brought it under arty and small arms fire.

A splinter injured my eye and the position became quite untenable. I disregarded the order to pull out, as this was clearly the best vantage point for me to conduct the shoot. Imagine the guns were engaging at such a rapid rate that one of the guns had its barrel explode. For nearly five days there was no sleep or rest and the discomfort becomes compounded when you throw in the height and the severe cold. The stress was telling to say the least. One mistake in your calculations and the ramifications would have been severe and unimaginable.'

I looked at the pictures Gurri had shared, of a get-together on the twenty-fifth anniversary of the Kargil War. He had been invited as a guest by the SF men he had supported during the attack and whose lives he had saved years ago on those frigid treacherous heights. Well, the SF are clannish and do not take to outsiders easily; the fact that he was invited is tribute and testament enough to what they thought of his contribution. As young men, Gurri and I had been part of a team that raised a Commando RR unit in Kashmir. Having seen him in action, I can say confidently, if a man was designed for the situation, the army would have been hard-pressed to find a more suitable candidate than Maj Gen Gurpreet Singh.

Though a lot of exceptionally fine leadership qualities can be gleaned from the above incident, i.e., courage, commitment, physical fitness, task focus, etc., I will limit myself to the ones I have not covered in some of the other accounts I have narrated. While Gurri in all humility talks about luck or divine intervention and no denying it played a huge hand, as it always does in most endeavours, I would prefer to call a large part of it competence. They do not post you as an instructor at the Arty school unless you are the 'crème de la crème' of the lot. And having served on the staff, as an ADC to the chief of the army, who was a gunner, I have first-hand experience of how professional and meticulous they were in the artillery. It is in the nature of their job. Often, when I was shoddy in some work, the brigadier would reprimand me with the words, 'Commando, you would have been sacked if you were a gunner by now. I would have taken your belt off in the gun pit.'

Competence or knowing your craft is an absolute given if subordinates are going to follow your orders/instructions. Mind you, there is a difference in half-heartedly following an order because you are the boss and following it with implicit trust in your knowledge and experience. This is because the quality of the work or the completion of a task may depend on this difference. And if you know your trade well, you can, if the occasion demands, be confident and qualified enough to improvise, take calculated risks and be ingenious.

Another aspect of leadership that I observed in some of the senior leaders I reported to both in the army and outside was their public speaking ability. All of them were confident speakers. The army understood the importance of this quality and spent a considerable amount of time, at various stages of your career, training you in the art of public speaking. Most early training courses that the young officers attend lays a lot of emphasis on how to conduct a training class or give various orders—for attack, defence, etc. In the SF, the orders were mostly limited to the nature of the job we were designed for, i.e., raid, ambush, reconnaissance, etc. and there was a standard format to be followed—the task, enemy information, own information, equipment and so on. The task was repeated twice and then someone in the team was asked to repeat. One of the critical things the instructors would mark you for was confidence, body language and optimism.

Imagine a leader, nervous, fluttering and stuttering while giving out attack orders where casualties are expected. What sort of confidence will he instil in the men he is going to lead? The battle is lost before commencement. Confidence or even a show of it and optimism are necessary in a leader. Mind you, confidence built on talent often leads to arrogance, while confidence built on discipline, hard work and preparation is always of a far deeper construct. Perpetual optimism is infectious and invigorating, however, there is a difference between being overly optimistic and being a realist. Certain situations demand a more realistic approach, especially during the planning stage. In fact, for military planning, a bit of pessimism aids in ensuring that the plan covers the shockers that may present themselves following Murphy's law, 'If there is a possibility of several things going wrong, the one that will go wrong is the one that will cause the most damage.'

Considering you commanded men from a diverse socio-economic milieu, especially in an SF unit, where men of all hues, drawn by a common aspiration, babbled in half a dozen different tongues, it was imperative that the language of orders be simplified for the ease of understanding. There was no attempt, unlike in the corporate world, to over-awe the men with high sounding buzzwords, fancy presentations and voluminous explanations. Everything was about simplicity, brevity and clarity. In my future life in the various companies I worked for, my department presentation was the simplest and the shortest. Good leaders are great simplifiers, reducing to essentials the complexities of the problem, making it easily understandable and identifiable to the rank and file.

The other quality I noticed in the army of my days and especially in the SF was the ability to plan the meagre resources we invariably had, especially when it came to equipment. For labour in our country is not always a crippling showstopper. Euphemistically called *jugaad* in Hindustani, or improvisation, is a typical Indian way of addressing scarcity or paucity of resources. It is the act of spontaneously performing or creating something, without any time for preparation or planning. Except, the Indian Army took it to the next level considering the harsh operating environment they must contend with. I recall lugging extra ammo and other control stores in condoms to protect them from water, or when for some time in Kashmir, we were carrying sanitary pads in lieu of the field dressing which was not available for gunshot wounds.

Rarely for a given task will you be granted your entire wish list. You just must make do with what is available. Else, where is the challenge if you are resource-rich? Anybody can do the job then. That is the reason Rommel is held in higher esteem for his generalship in the Africa campaign than his opponent, Montgomery, despite being defeated in battle by the latter. Monty had overwhelming superiority in arms, equipment and manpower. In the end, leadership is multifaceted and context-dependent. I have seen some of my seniors, both in the army and outside, often display various aspects of leadership in different situations. Some very hands-off bosses could, if the occasion demanded, very comfortably roll up their sleeves and pitch in with the team. There were others who were purely transactional and would often struggle in a situation where a change of leadership style was demanded. Leadership is an evolving art—a blend of audacity, empathy, decisiveness and adaptability. Whether in combat or in a business environment, the essence of leadership lies in the ability to inspire through action, to listen and adjust. Clear concise articulation, resource planning and competence in your craft go a long way in establishing your leadership.

Takeaways

- ***Leadership is earned, not conferred.*** *Rank gives authority on paper; real leadership is built by conduct, competence and the trust you win from your men.*
- ***Serve before you command.*** *Small acts—tasting the food, checking the toilets, shaking a sweeper's hand—reveal a leader's priorities and earn respect.*
- ***Humour is a force-multiplier.*** *Timely levity in misery or danger sustains morale, humanises command and diffuses tension.*
- ***Detach emotion for hard calls.*** *Making decisions based on facts and rational analysis, rather than personal emotions or biases, leads to fair and effective outcome.*
- ***Flex your persona—theatre has its uses.*** *The skilful leader switches between host, disciplinarian, raconteur or bully (if necessary) to read and move an audience.*
- ***Lead from the front when it matters.*** *Presence in crisis—*

rolling up sleeve and sharing risk—inspires loyalty and steadies execution.

- ***Execution is non-negotiable—finish the job.*** *Delivering tasks fully and without compromise reflects dedication and sets a standard for excellence.*
- ***Improvise and adapt—practise situational leadership.*** *Make do with scarce resources (*jugaad*), balance audacity with realism and shift between servant, transactional or transformational styles as the moment demands.*

GREEN ON—GO!

When it feels scary to jump, that is exactly when you jump. Otherwise, you end up staying in the same place your whole life.

–An old paratrooper

It is the crack of dawn and bitterly cold, as we help each other up on our feet and trudge up the ramp like space men, weighed down heavily with the main and the reserve parachutes. I am with my troop of 20 men in Agra to do our mandatory annual refresher jumps. I am the last man in my stick and would be the first out of the door—an unwritten rule amongst the airborne forces, whereby the senior-most man is invariably expected to lead in any risky or life-threatening venture. The Indian Army overall inculcates into its leaders the motto, 'follow me'. At the door, I cast a furtive glance at the tall eucalyptus trees at the periphery of the tarmac to gauge the winds. It is blustery for sure and would be blowing harder at a thousand-plus feet. I turn my attention to the starboard stick and see an unusual sight.

It is a troop of men from the PBG (President's Bodyguards). Every man is well over six feet, heavy set and some with impressive moustaches, towering over the few men from my team, who had been interspersed with them in the stick. The PBG are members of the last of the cavalry units still existing in the world. While their role is purely ceremonial, each man is an expert horseman and a qualified paratrooper. On parade, astride their big steeds, they are a heartening sight to watch. But here, in the cramped fuselage of an AN-32, weighed down with the chutes, their necks bent, shuffling ungainly along, they look wretched, like a column of condemned men walking to the gallows. And for some, it was practically just that.

Their dismayed expressions showed the torment each man was going through. Their senior NCO (non-commissioned officer) had confessed to me before emplaning that some of the men in this bunch had not jumped in a decade or so. This was the lot which had managed to dodge the mandatory annual jumps on some pretext or the other and had finally been corralled and packed off to earn their jump allowance. If you are heavy, parachuting is not a very pleasant experience since you tend to hit the ground harder. And the wind gods were not being kind today.

My stick was the first to exit and having hit terra firma, I promptly rolled my chute and stood around watching as the aircraft banked and steadied to disgorge the other half of its human load. One, two, three, I counted, as the jumpers hit the slipstream and were propelled out violently and then a longish pause. Someone had clearly hesitated and I made a mental note to find out if it was one of my men. Later, as I neared the rendezvous, my attention was drawn to loud angry voices emanating from behind the building. I turned the corner and saw a confrontation in the offing, with my men drawn up on one side and the PBG guys on the other; Girwar, a black belt from my team, verbally pitching into this enormous PBG trooper.

The numbers were equally matched, but physically they were practically double our size. My first thought was, what a joke it would be in the regiment that a bunch of horsemen beat up an SF team. I would never be able to live it down. But then I noticed that all the aggression was from my boys, while the bulk of the PBG men just stood around timidly, as Girwar berated the big man in the choicest of expletives.

'All right, simmer down,' I said, 'what is the issue?'

'This big oaf is a coward,' replied Girwar angrily. 'Everything was going fine. I was number four in the stick and behind this mountain of lard, when he suddenly came to the door and stopped. Then he just sat down, dangling his legs like a girl on a swing. I had to finally jump over him and messed up my exit. Most of us in the stick behind him fell outside the drop zone. Someone could have gotten hurt. Now, he calls himself a Rajput and so am I. He is a disgrace to his clan and his uniform and he must shave those moustaches now, or I will do it for him.'

I looked at the man for an explanation. He thought briefly, demurred and then in an apologetic tone answered, 'I do not know how to explain, *sahib.* I am jumping after many years. My mind was playing havoc throughout, conjuring up doomsday images and when I came to the exit, I briefly hesitated. The longer I stood there, the more rooted I became to the spot. I could not convince myself why I was doing what I was doing, especially when I disliked it so much. Then my legs started trembling and I sat down. Maybe, I should not have thought so much.'

Clearly, the men were not swallowing this excuse, but I could relate to his experience. Often, I had stood as the lead man on the stick, looking down into a pitch-black howling night, heavily loaded with all the paraphernalia of war and wondering what the hell was I doing there. Inner turmoil can grip even the most battle-hardened soldiers when the mind struggles against the gravity of risk. It was, however, a great lesson for me. His moment of indecision underscored for me the necessity of decisive action under stress—a lesson that came in handy to me soon when put to test in combat. The big man, like me, clearly had a fertile imagination, except for the difference that often separates the doer from the procrastinator. Imagination is a great virtue to have if channelised constructively. If allowed to run riot, it can create havoc with the mind. Fear is one of the by-products of it and useful if it sharpens your senses and is not disproportionate to the degree of danger. Unfettered fear can overwhelm and render you irrational, susceptible to the fight-or-flight syndrome. This incident then naturally led me into a broader reflection on the anatomy of fear.

The amygdala is a part of the brain that detects threats and activates proper fear-related behaviour in response to any life-threatening stimulus. As Christoper McDougall explains in his book *The Natural Born Heroes,* the amygdala accesses your past memory bank to scan if what you are about to do has been done in the past. If there is a match, you go about the act with minimum disruption to your breathing, heart rate and anxiousness. But if it does not detect a similar past experience, it will command the nervous system to shun away from the dangerous act. The amygdala does not reason, but it responds and therefore can only be trained and not deceived to revoke the reaction to resist a threat. This is the reason the SF believe in realistic training. As the song by Rodgers and Hart goes, 'Things you do, come back to you, as though they knew the way.' This understanding of fear sets the stage for realistic and daunting training scenarios in the SF.

One of the situations the SF trains for is a room or building intervention. It takes a lot of courage to enter a room, knowing there is a man waiting to inflict grievous harm on you and is prepared to die in the bargain. Despite all the training, the first man in through the door goes on a wing and a prayer. It is a leap of faith, often called the *funnel of death* in army jargon. The leap of faith refers to risk-taking in a situation where you step into the unknown, without enough certainty of success, purely with the hope that things will work out fine. It is instinct-

and belief-based and lacks concrete evidence. If poised against the wall, just before the door is kicked in or blown open with explosives, you allow your mind to vacillate and wander on the dark side, the chances are you will dither, a consequence of which could be fatal. I had a personal experience of how the brain, or specifically the amygdala, functions in such life-threatening situations.

An infantry battalion in Sri Lanka had been mauled badly, suffering severe casualties including their commanding officer and the SM. Two SF teams were flown in to stabilise and sanitise the situation. Well-versed with the Indian Army's SOP in such scenarios, the Tamil Tigers knew that SF's troops would now fly in. A party of theirs encamped at night across the post on a hillock in anticipation of further air activity. The aim was to down a chopper, ideally packed with its human cargo. However, things went awry, as often they do when put to the test of battle, especially the best-conceived plans, which strangely are more vulnerable to the perils of Murphy's law: 'In any field of endeavour, anything that can go wrong, will go wrong.'

In their hastily prepared opportunity ambush, they forgot one essential standard operating procedure the Indians always followed before the commencement of any air activity: the sanitisation of the helipad. A helipad protection party of ten men inadvertently blundered into the well-concealed LTTE militants, compelling them to open fire prematurely. The protection party, caught in the open, lost five men; but the sacrifice was not in vain since it alerted the post and a lively firefight ensued. If five Indian mothers lost their sons that day, it saved a lot of other mothers from mourning the loss of their sons. Had surprise not been lost, there is no telling of the loss we would have suffered if they had succeeded in bagging a chopper full of men. It turned into a classic small arms engagement, with mortars and RPGs adding to the din.

The brigade commander's briefing was in progress when all hell broke loose on the post. Anyway, I was ordered to collect my men and take stock of the situation. I took cover behind a temple wall, wondering what I could possibly do in this hail of incoming fire. I was young, inexperienced, coming under fire for the first time and this was a completely alien situation. The thought that I could die made my mind inert to a clear assessment of the action needed. A perfect scenario, you will agree, and tailor-made for my brain to resist taking any risky action. While I had received my usual military training, never had I been at the receiving end of fire which could kill me. The amygdala did a quick scan of my memory bank to relay back to my nervous system that no such high-risk experience had been detected. It promptly ordered my nervous system to shut down and cease any foolhardy risk from being taken.

I dithered, cowering behind the wall, when the CO, Col PC Katoch (later retired as a Lt Gen), walked up and sharply told me in a calm voice to assault the hillock where he could see enemy movement. The moment I stepped out of cover, a burst of gunfire erupted from the thick foliage of a tree barely 30 metres away. It was close enough for me to extend a hand and collect the lead. Self-preservation overwhelmed any training I had had for the occasion and I promptly stepped back behind the wall. Clearly, the Tamil Tigers had placed a man to cut off any troops from slipping out of the post.

The team commander behind was screaming something about taking a detour and Satish, my point man breathing down my neck, was not helping by poking me in the ribs with his AK barrel and urging me to take the lead. It was one of those occasions where reputations are made or tarnished forever. The orders were clear, the inclination to follow them existing; however, courage oscillated like a pendulum, and with the noise of the battle, the fog of war, my mind retreated into numb stupefaction. Then, with a herculean effort of will, I dashed out of cover. I guess, any healthy young man would have done the same in similar circumstances, or in all probability the training I had received helped. Hesitation in the face of risk is a luxury one cannot afford in the SF. The same principle applies off the battlefield. We managed a kill or two in that engagement. In retrospect, if I had not taken that leap of faith, mentally I would still be cowering behind that wall for the rest of my life. Where risk is, deliverance also beckons.

Now I come to the point I am trying to make from the above-mentioned anecdotes. When you come to the Rubicon, you don't go fishing. You cross it. While the incidents mentioned are clearly life-threatening in varying degrees, there would be occasions in your personal or professional life where you have deliberated and taken a decision, but hesitated to take the plunge. A delayed or no decision is worse than a wrong one. In the latter case, you will know over time the mistakes you made and can take the necessary corrective action. But sitting on the fence and waiting to see which way the wind blows is a huge disservice you do to yourself. While you get temporary relief, in all probability the crisis/situation, given time, will only bloat in size, with far more profound consequences. Murphy sums it aptly: 'Left to themselves, things always go from bad to worse.'

I am tempted to quote John Ruskin: 'This I know, that if you come to a dangerous place and turn back from it, though it may have been perfectly right and wise to do so, still your character has suffered some slight deterioration; you are to that extent weaker, more lifeless, more effeminate, more liable to passion and error in future; whereas if you go through with the danger, though it may have been apparently rash and foolish to encounter it, you come out of the encounter a stronger and a better man, fitter for every sort of work and trial and nothing but danger produces this effect.'

While Ruskin uses the word *danger*, the overarching precept of what he writes however stays the same; to turn back at the point of commitment only diminishes you as a person. A series of such reversals in big or small decisions of life has the potential overtime to become a habit. One quickly learns to justify such setbacks, convincing oneself that the reasons were justifiable and things could have only gone worse if the decision taken had been carried through. This leads to untold and prolonged misery sometimes, with no remedial action available later.

Bertolt Brecht mentions, 'Because things are the way they are, things will not stay the way they are.' A delayed decision, in the hope of more clarity or reduction in risk, will invariably heighten the risk. It is understandable that some of the decisions may not be easy and may involve a high degree of risk or uncertainty. Everybody's risk thresholds are different and may vary from situation to situation, that is, personal, professional, moral, etc. As General Colin Powell mentions in his book *It worked For Me,* one of the ways to ease decision making is to work out a personal risk probability ratio. However, depending on the criticality of the issue, the risk probability ratio may be tweaked a bit, but the operating thresholds must be adhered to. Personally, I limit myself within a 60–70 per cent range. For example, if I have 60 or 70 per cent information, I will take a call, rather than wait for 100 per cent clarity, which may or may never happen. Invariably, the quality and quantity of information available is inversely proportional to the criticality of the event. The more important the matter, the lesser information you seem to own.

In the build-up to the raid which killed Osama bin Laden in Pakistan, other than the method, the more critical question was the absolute confirmation that the shadowy figure seen walking in the backyard of the targeted house was Osama and not some unknown man keeping a low profile for any number of reasons. The implications of getting this information wrong were colossal, affecting not only the longevity of the American president's office for one, but the risk of national humiliation and the extreme risk the raiding force ran, entering a friendly country and getting into an unequal gunfight. Some of the experts and sceptics in the planning team put the probability ratio at 50–60 per cent, and it is to the credit of President Barack Obama that he gave the green signal for the op. Sometimes fortune favours the brave.

Fear or an inability to be decisive in a life-threatening or life-changing situation is a response of an individual's instinct of self-preservation to danger or to the anticipated consequences expected in the aftermath of the decision. As the saying goes, 'For those who take risks, life has a flavour the sheltered never know of.' No risk–no reward is the greatest incentive to subdue fear of the unknown. In both personal and professional life, embracing risks is essential to get breakthroughs, innovate, solve problems and creative novel ideas that would never happen through a cautious approach. It leads to personal growth and resilience and bolsters your confidence in challenging times. No one understood the risk–reward game better than Major Sudhir Walia, Ashok Chakra and SM (Bar). But unfortunately, he is not around to expound his theory on the subject. He was killed in action years ago in the very engagement for which he got the AC (posthumously).

Often when our paths crossed in the violence-torn valley of yesteryears, he would regale me with his many narrow escapes.

In his time, he had already made a reputation for taking high risks, which reflected in the many militants he and his team annihilated. When I once cautioned him to tread carefully, he just laughed and said they were all calculated risks. One cannot kill someone whose intent is to kill you without taking a certain amount of risk. In one of the podcasts, I was asked about it and I recall mentioning that high risks come with high rewards, which any punter in the financial markets will tell you, except that in the army, you trade in lives.

While in the former, if you get the risk evaluation wrong and lady luck abandons you, the maximum you lose is your capital or your job. However, in combat, if you read the risks wrong and the stars are not aligned with you at that moment, well, you could end up losing your life or getting maimed. And luck is an unreliable element to lean on too much, or too often. I am conscious that my examples are all extreme, involving life and death situations, but then so was the profession where I served as a young man. The perceptive reader can draw their own conclusions about how they relate to a less dangerous existence in their professional and personal life. A personal incident comes to mind, elucidating the difference in approach between individuals in such demanding situations.

It is two in the morning; there is heavy snow on the ground and the temperature is well below zero. I am leading with my troop and another officer from a sister SF unit brings up the rear with his men. It is a joint op somewhere in the Lolab Valley in north Kashmir. The plan is simple: to hit the village of Dardpura and ensconce the entire party before daylight in a couple of houses. Thereafter, wait for militant movement to begin, back and forth between the village and their lairs somewhere up the mountain. There is intelligence of a heavily armed bunch of foreign *mujahideen* who have been regularly haunting the hamlet. Dardpura had a nasty reputation, for a battalion strength op had to be called off once, as the militants engaged the troops from the surrounding hills with accurate small arms and machine gun fire.

As we were running slow and daylight beckoned, it was decided to stick together and make the mosque in the centre of the village the base. At dawn, the first call to prayer rang out to the faithful. In that snowbound stillness of the village, the Arabic words resounded loud and clear, with a mesmerising power to galvanise the believer to hasten to his maker. Just then the sniper perched on the minaret, reported seeing a figure emerge from the forest about 400 yards away. Permission to engage was refused, as we thought he maybe the lead scout and the main party would be following behind.

The man sat at the edge of the forest, intently surveying the village below. Perhaps the militants were planning to come down to the mosque to offer the day's first *namaz*. Then, ten minutes later, the man got up and retreated into the forest. Clearly, someone in the village must have signalled our presence. Anyway, an hour later we realised the game was up and decided to head home. The wizened old *mulla* was standing around and I asked him in conversation if he had any idea about the whereabouts of the hideouts in the forest. I was pleasantly surprised when he nodded his head in acknowledgement.

'Well, will you lead us to the place?' I asked.

'I am not stupid enough to do something like that, but I can show you.'

With that, he took us to the side of the mosque and showed a set of boot marks in the hard snow heading towards the mountain. We walked with him to the edge of the forest. Pointing to the boot marks going up the hill and disappearing into the forest, he said, 'Just follow the footsteps, *jenab*. Where they end, you are bound to run into its owner. Pay attention *huzoor*, for he is not alone and they are bound to give you a warm reception. *Khuda hafiz*.'

Both the officers now stood behind a tree to discuss the next plan of action. Somewhere up there in the swirling mist were an indeterminate number of militants. I looked at the other officer junior to me, but with more operational experience in the valley.

'Well, Pandit*ji*,' I said, 'we could split up and take it from the flanks. But it is going to be an uphill fight, and you cannot manoeuvre as the snow is going to be waist high in places.'

'Agree, sir. And the weather is packing up. If we have casualties, forget about choppers. We also have no idea of their strength and with this mist rolling in, finding their hideout is going to be a problem. Surprise is lost in any case. But you are the senior. *Hukam do* (give orders).'

'While I am the senior, Pandit*ji*,' I replied defensively, 'you are the one with the experience. What do you say then?'

And so on and so forth went the discussion, with all sorts of dismal and bleak views being presented by both of us, till we convinced ourselves that it was foolhardy to try something which clearly guaranteed casualties. Now, right or wrong, sensible to abort or a wasted opportunity are not the questions here. I narrate the incident because I know for certain that there are friends of mine, well some long dead now, who would not have hesitated a second to ponder the question: to be or not to be. And Sudhir Walia was one of them, a highly decorated SF officer who had a reputation for taking enormous risks in combat and was later killed in action. There are confirmed militants somewhere up yonder, so what is there to discuss? The only way is to go forward and deal with them. Period.

Great leaders and successful people understand the risk–reward cycle and are not averse to taking hard calls, knowing fully well that failure and success are not permanent and often one follows the other. As mentioned earlier, however, risk thresholds differ from individual to individual and it is not necessary that someone who can take high personal risks will also be the kind to play high stakes in his financial or personal dealings. Limiting myself to the ability to take risks involved in soldiering, it all depends on how you address it in your head.

My belief is that too much pessimism, scepticism, negativity or a lack of confidence in temperament does not lend itself well to take high risks.

In the end, it boils down to taming the mind and controlling the negative chatter. Temperamentally, it is a great boon to be an optimist when it comes to taking tough decisions, especially where risk of any kind is concerned. But if you are given to gloomy thoughts, which often hold you back from taking the leap, then you need to discipline your mind. The more you train or prepare for a particular nasty or risky situation, the fainter are the voices of doom. The mind rid of unnecessary bleak thoughts can then focus better on the job at hand. Consequently, the decision, product or conduct of a calm mind is always going to be better. Professional mixed martial arts (MMA) coaches will tell you that given a choice between an aggressive fighter and a calm one, the preference would be for the latter. Thomas Hardy very precisely nailed it when he said, 'More life may trickle out of men through thought than through a gaping wound.'

The scourge of anxiety and depression so prevalent today is often a consequence of a person's inability to tame the dark thoughts from allowing them to take ominous proportions. I call it the mountains of the mind. There were so many occasions where, before stepping out for an operation, I would be assailed with all sorts of dismal thoughts ending in my getting shot—the price one pays for having a fertile imaginative mind. But then I reasoned out rationally the chances of your getting killed, the position you hold, your reputation, etc., and in the end, with a bit of fatalism, I did what I was trained and paid to do. Seneca sums it beautifully in a line, 'We suffer more in our imagination than in reality.' I had a young soldier under my charge in Sri Lanka. One night, while on sentry duty, he shot his index finger, claiming it to be accidental. I, along with the senior JCO, questioned him and concluded that he had done it on purpose. In his panicked state, he had made the mistake of blowing up his trigger finger, needing a discharge from service. Malingering is not uncommon in highly volatile combat situations, but this man was a first-class soldier and had shown no signs so far of shirking action. When told he would be discharged, he opened with his plea bargain, confessing he had done it deliberately to get some relief from the constant pressure of going out on combat patrols, as lately he was prone to panic attacks and bouts of anxiety. A voice, he claimed, was telling him his time was up. There was an old saying in the British army during WWI, 'When a man is at war, his mind should be at peace.' No man's courage is unlimited and eventually he will crack, depending on how much he draws on it. Constant exposure to danger, monotony of existence, physical exhaustion, separation from family or any number of things can weaken the mind. In his case, it was also the wrong attitude to danger which had brought him to this state.

There is a delicate balance between fear of the unknown and the necessity of overcoming it to embrace risk and drive personal growth. While fear is a natural response to uncertainty, it can also be a barrier to progress. By controlling our minds and reframing fear as an opportunity for growth, we can transform apprehension into action. The metaphor of 'green-on—go!', mentioned as the heading to the chapter, suggests adopting a mindset that signals readiness to move forward despite uncertainties. This approach to certain situations in life encourages individuals to take calculated risks, which are essential for innovation and personal development. Without such proactive steps, there is a risk of remaining stagnant, metaphorically staying in the same place throughout one's life. Thus, the key lies in acknowledging fear, controlling our responses and taking informed risks to foster growth and avoid stagnation—figuratively speaking, of course.

Mark Twain puts it across very succinctly when he says, 'I am an old man and have known a great many troubles. But most of them never happened.' A very relatable saying and a lot of us will recall events in our life where you prepared yourself for the worst-case scenario and were pleasantly surprised when things unfolded very differently. Hitchcock puts the same point across a little differently and I quote; 'There is no terror in the bang; only in the anticipation of it.' How true. The anticipation of something unpleasant which is expected stresses you more than the actual event eventually.

The challenge always is to anchor the mind to the present moment, for to be everywhere is to be nowhere. Professional seasoned soldiers understand the frailty of the mind and its power to conjure up adverse scenarios and were therefore keenly aware that danger existed only at a certain place and time and not before or after. They were not given to anxiety or stress, were good in combat and carried very few emotional scars in its aftermath. 'The wise soldier lives for the hour,' as they said for soldiers in the First World War. Perhaps they followed Seneca, who has the following to comment on the subject; 'To be ready for everything. If I am let off in anyway, I am pleased. The day in question proves me wrong in a sense, if it treats me leniently, but ever so not really wrong, for just as I know that anything is capable of happening, so also do I know that it is not bound to happen. So, I look for the best and am prepared for the opposite.' He is trying to convey the mind's resilience to handle the difficulties of life—to conduct life positively, while being still conscious of the uncertainties that life may throw at you at any moment.

Good combat soldiers, I noticed, embraced the troublesome situation they were in and went about addressing it with a fair dose of fatalism—'If it is written by a higher power, nothing can erase the fate that awaits me; so why mull it so much?' I guess it would be easier to combat the negative noises in the mind if one understood the intervention of luck in most things human; the differentiating factor lies in how everyone perceives the given situation and reacts then accordingly.

Depending on your luck, 10 to 20 per cent of the time they say, the cards are often dealt out to you. The difference between winners and losers inherently exists in how one reacts to the given situation. As an example, you are heading to the airport and run into a traffic jam. It is bumper to bumper and you know missing the flight is a forgone conclusion. Most folks start wallowing in self-pity, getting anxious and cursing their luck. The winner is the man who swiftly realises the situation is beyond his capability to alter, so pointless to fret over it. Some situations, to use a word from the legal parlance, are *force majeure*. The positive person takes a quick decision to book the next ticket and moves on. A simple example, but it conveys the point of not expanding unnecessary mind space, hoping the situation will resolve itself in time or sitting around cursing your misfortune. If I were to relate positivity with happiness and happy people are positive or vice-versa, then as per psychologists (Lyubomirsky, Sheldon & Schkade (2005), 50 per cent is genetics, 10 per cent circumstances and the remaining 40 per cent is attitude or mindset. Even if you were unfortunate enough to inherit a negative, unhappy disposition from your parents, you are still the master of the remaining 50 per cent. It is not a precise science and its real value empowers you to focus on what you can control—your intentional actions. 'For happiness cannot be pursued; it must ensue,' as Frankl believed.

While thinking is fine, overthinking in any situation is highly detrimental, if not a complete waste. Some wise guy worked out that the average human has approximately 40,000 thoughts a day and out of that, nearly 80 per cent are repeat thoughts of the earlier past two days—a gross waste of mind space and constructive thinking. The animal world has a better comprehension of this concept of overthinking. Watch a hunt on the grasslands of an African wildlife sanctuary—an attack by a pride of lions or a cheetah, the alarmed scattering of the gazelle herd, the chase and the kill. Within minutes of the kill, the scene is back to normal, the herd reverts to grazing as if they never lost a member of their herd. Wild animals only run from danger they see or smell and once they escape, they worry no more.

Let me touch upon another consequence of this constant unproductive negative chatter in the head. The other day, my wife, peering over the newspaper, turned to me and read out a news snippet about a young CEO who collapsed on the treadmill while running and passed away because of a heart attack. The others in the room chimed in with various other such examples of people dying young because of heart failure. The unanimous opinion was stress—a global scourge which is ailing the young, especially the high-profile individuals and clearly brought upon primarily by heightened pressure at the workplace it appears. This is also the reason so many companies spend time and energy to achieve the so-called mythical work–life balance. Mythical I say, because human nature follows the Malthusian theory of diminishing returns. Too much tilt towards one factor, life balance, while keeping the other factor, work, constant will eventually result in a progressive decline in output and employee satisfaction.

'What pressure?' I retorted. 'Every job has its pressures which are directly proportional to the rewards. The defence services, I guess being the only exception to that rule in a sense. The more the pressure to deliver, the more financial package you get. After all, they will not lose their lives; they are not fighting a bloody war.'

This led to a healthy discussion around professional stress the young today are expected to handle. My mind switched off as I briefly drifted to another place, another time.

A fighting patrol is struggling up a mountain in the Pir Panjal range in J&K in atrocious weather and a pitch-black night. In a vicious thunderstorm, the men hold each other as they haul themselves up to hit the thickly forested ridge line at 8000 feet. At first light, the incessant rain takes a pause, as the shadows in the nooks and corners of the trees gently start to fade. Under the canopy of the forest, however, the last vestige of the night still lingers. A log fire flickers through the undergrowth at a distance, its faint crackling carrying across to us, as the flames pick up from time to time, on receiving a gust of wind blowing through the forest. We close in to investigate. It is bandit country and no villagers are going to be camping in the middle of the forest in this kind of weather.

Stealthily, we creep closer, and standing behind a tree, I spy a few people sitting around the fire. Suddenly, the stillness of the forest is shattered by the loud report of automatic gunfire at close range. My next view is of my buddy lying next to me, with a thin trickle of blood oozing down his throat. He is muttering my name, so I know the injury is superficial and he is fine. But when I look towards the fire, it takes my breath away. Two of the locals are lying in the fire with head shots and a third has rolled over on the side with multiple gunshots. My lead scout has crashed into the thicket, shot through his waist and another round has smashed his elbow. It is grade A carnage and a scene straight out of a horror film.

Anyway, we haul our man—badly mauled and barely breathing—and lug him down the mountain on our backs. Despite our best efforts, he succumbed to his injuries twenty days later in the hospital. I am redeployed to the valley for further operations. Then, about a month later, I received sudden orders to report back—I have been attached to an RR unit pending a court of inquiry into the incident. But that is just the beginning. Because the area was not officially declared a 'disturbed zone' under AFSPA, the civil authorities decided to make an example. A police FIR is lodged against me, accusing me of multiple homicides. To add to the fire, the National Human Rights Commission (NHRC) initiates a parallel investigation. At this point, I am wedged—firmly and hopelessly—between a rock and a hard place. Worst of all, I am not even sure which way is up.

Worst case scenario—I get convicted and land up in jail, other than a court martial from the service that will follow. And while the evidence is collected and a verdict reached, I am sent back to lead men into combat. Now that is what I call professional stress. And there are enough people around I know, with more hair-raising experiences to narrate. None collapsed because of stress-caused heart failure.

But it is difficult to explain to the uninitiated. This yawning gap in handling stress that exists between the average person and someone who has had unusual rough experiences often leads to me being labelled insensitive by my family. I am reminded of an article I read years ago in *Reader's Digest*, while it was still in publication, written by someone who was an ex-bomber pilot during the Second World War. The man, after the war, is travelling with his wife and two daughters in a car for a holiday. Suddenly, a large bee slips in and as is the way with caged insects, starts buzzing around angrily to escape captivity. There is pandemonium as the three females scream and scramble around the car to get out of the way of the now equally frightened and agitated bee.

In all this bedlam, the man calmly continues driving. When the bee is finally evicted and normalcy returns, the three ladies pounce on him for his callousness and indifference to the crisis. He opens his mouth to defend himself and then decides on silence. How can he explain what it was to be flying over Germany, with the flak exploding around you and the German fighters weaving and tearing through your formation? An engine on fire, a gaping hole in the fuselage and a couple of dead and wounded gunners on board, trusting you to fly the limping B-52 back to base. The casualty rate was often as high as 60 per cent.

The anecdotes elaborate the point I am making—stress is a creation of the mind and a strong mind is capable of containing the negative chatter that is bound to flare up in any ugly situation. For a combat soldier, it is not during, but after a traumatic ordeal that the stress kicks in, referred to now as the post-traumatic stress disorder (PTSD). Of course, the experiences in the SF prepared you thoroughly to handle extreme stress. What can be more stressful than losing a limb or life? If as a person you are predisposed to veer more towards the negative side of thinking, the attempt should be to train the mind to first lessen negative thinking and inculcate more positive thinking if possible. In other words, if you cannot always be positive, or train yourself to be a positive person, the least you can do is to reduce the negative thoughts. This will reduce the stress which comes from constant negative chatter in the head.

As mentioned earlier in the chapter, in sustained high-pressure situations, fatalism often helps to sustain the mind from losing its grip on the present. There is much truth in the saying, 'Que sera, sera' (whatever will be, will be).

Most combat soldiers somewhere deep down are fatalistic, believing firmly that when your time has come to greet your maker, nothing can alter the course. This simple conviction often helps a soldier cope with the perils in his profession. Over time, one realises that only effort is in your hands and not the consequences. *Maktub,* as the Arabs say—it is written. My father would often say, if I cribbed about my bad luck, '*Waqt ke pehley aur naseeb se zyada, na kisi ko mila hai aur na milega*' (Nobody will get his dues before his time or more than what is in his destiny). Now, I am conscious when I make this statement, for there are folks out there who believe in charting their own destiny. Everything is in your hands, they will tell you. Well, not really. You could imagine so for the time being, perhaps if you have got your returns on effort. Well, I am a firm supporter of hard work and it is certainly not a moot point. But as for creating your own destiny, I am reminded of an anecdote.

Years ago, when the devil's wind was blowing across the Kashmir valley and independence from the Indian state beckoned, all sorts of young men went across to Pakistan to get trained and armed, to come back and unleash mayhem in the state. Of all these young men, one of them fell foul to our guns early in his *jehadi* career. He clearly was different and seemed to be a true revolutionary with an ideology. In his rucksack, we found a diary with all his thoughts and views. But most of the writing was poetry, good stuff at that, and I quoted a couplet or two from his work in my first novel.

Anyway, on his AK-47, he had with coloured stickers written a couplet, which thereafter became our unit's maxim of sorts and found a permanent place in our ops room. He was a sensitive, educated youngster and perhaps marked out by the seniors as a potential future leader. But fortunately for us, he was a better poet than a militant and died believing in a quote he cherished dearly enough to carry it around on his weapon.

Noor-e-haq shamma illahi ko bujha sakta hai kaun,
Jiska hami ho khuda, usko mita sakta hai kaun
(Oh, who can extinguish Allah's flame,
And how can anyone be harmed,
If Allah stands to protect his name).

Age and hard experience over time have taught me that hesitation borne from an overactive imagination and self-preservation can often paralyse the best of men. Embracing risks, despite their inherent dread, tackling fear boldly and controlling negativity is essential for personal growth and professional success. Remember that the moments when you have chosen to jump are the ones when you should jump.

Takeaways

- ***A fertile imagination is a gift—but only when tethered to purpose.*** *Let your mind roam, but guide it with discipline. Untamed imagination breeds anxiety. Directed imagination fuels strategy, innovation and foresight.*
- ***Fear is not the enemy—it is a signal.*** *Understand it, harness it and convert it into heightened awareness. Fear, when well-managed, sharpens instincts and preserves clarity.*
- ***Every task, no matter how small or mighty, demands mental rehearsal and practical groundwork.*** *Define timelines. Break them into achievable milestones. You don't rise to the occasion—you fall to the level of your preparation.*
- ***Timely decisions trump perfect ones.*** *A bad decision can be course-corrected. Indecision is paralysis. In high-stakes situations, momentum matters. Keep moving.*
- ***Know your personal risk threshold.*** *Identify the level of uncertainty you can absorb. This mental metric simplifies*

choices and saves time in the fog of crisis. Not every hill is worth dying on—know which ones are.

- ***Failure and success are both temporary guests.*** *Do not chase one or run from the other. Learn. Adapt. Repeat. What matters is your ability to stay the course, not the occasional spike or stumble.*
- ***Understand the risk-reward equation.*** *Every decision is a wager. Calculate the upside. Acknowledge the downside. Then leap, if it is worth it. Courage is not the absence of risk—it is clarity in the face of it.*
- ***Control the mind, or it will control you.*** *Negative inner chatter can be more lethal than external threats. Learn to observe your thoughts without obeying them.*
- ***Contingency readiness is not paranoia—it is professionalism.*** *Life throws surprises. Be mentally primed for chaos. Have fallback plans. Train your mind to flex, not fracture, in the face of the unexpected.*
- ***Live in the now. Stay situationally aware.*** *Distraction is a danger. Stay rooted in the present moment, attuned to shifts in your environment. Whether it is a boardroom or battlefield—clarity comes from presence.*
- ***Stress is not your enemy—mishandling it is.*** *Stress reveals, it does not destroy—unless you let it. Build mental endurance through deliberate exposure, self-reflection and recovery rituals. A strong mind is not born—it is built.*
- ***Perfect work-life balance is a myth—find your own***

personal equation. *Some situations demand more of work, others more of life. The key is conscious trade-offs. You do not balance—you choose what matters, when it matters.*

- ***Yes, luck and destiny exist. But grit can balance them both.*** *Luck is a factor. So is timing. But neither should ever write your story. Keep showing up. Keep moving forward. Dreams are not granted—they are earned.*

NO ONE CAN MOTIVATE YOU LIKE YOU CAN

If a job is worth doing, then it is worth doing with everything you have got.

–Anonymous

Often, I have been invited, by virtue of the fact that I served in the army, to give a motivational talk to the employees of some company or the other. In the introduction to this book, I mention the reasons for my reluctance to espouse the subject. In my entire service with the SF, I recall only two instances where a motivational or pep talk, as it is called in the army, was given. The first was while we were in Sri Lanka, when a LTTE camp in the jungle was to be hit, and another, in different circumstances, back at the unit base in India. Unlike what has been portrayed in the Hindi movie *Uri*, where before heading off for a mission, the leader shouts, 'How's the *josh*?' and in unison the body of men reply, 'High, sir,' in reality, the mission commander will do a quick random check of the gear and equipment, repeat the order of march, last minute instructions and share a few scenarios that may play out.

In fact, if anything, it was just the opposite in Sri Lanka, where before stepping out of the post on a mission at night, there would be whispered instructions, a quick radio check, a murmur of the unit's war cry, with the only ominous, resounding and strident note being of the weapons being cocked and loaded. Well, the idea is not to bust the myth of a good pep talk. I am sure, sometime, somewhere, for some people on the right occasion, it helps raise morale and motivation. But it is very fleeting and task-specific. Regular pep talks do not sustain an elevated level of motivation in the team, especially over an extended period. Motivation must be looked for within and not outside. True motivation is not delivered; it is discovered, and often, under duress. Let me narrate a personal anecdote.

It is the spring of 1989 in Sri Lanka and two SF teams have been flown to an IPKF post in preparation for an incursion into the LTTE-infested jungles, to hit one of their main camps.

The briefing for the mission wraps up and the two majors decide to give a bit of a pep talk if it could be called one. It has been nearly three decades, but the scene is indelibly etched in my mind. I may not remember the exact words, but the gist of the talk was the following.

'You know the orders we have received and they are stupid. Nevertheless, orders are orders and will be followed. Now, those of you who were present in a similar op, when we hit the camp in Mutur, know the casualties we bought. This camp is much bigger, and as per intelligence, the number two man in the hierarchy, Mahattaya, may be around. If he is there, the Black Tigers are surely going to be with him for protection. They are going to fight tooth and nail. More importantly, the bloody jungle is going to be mined and booby trapped. Be careful about the IEDs (improvised explosive devices), especially up in the trees. Be prepared, since legs and hands will fly. If any of you is wounded, for God's sake do not make a racket. It draws fire. We will try and get to you if we can. Else go to your maker peacefully. Remember, you came to us of your own volition, we did not ask for you, and do not forget you are the tip of the spear and the best the army has. If there is trouble, well, fight it out. There is no cavalry coming to bail you out. Finish with your wills and letters and get some sleep and food. If I know the army, we might be in for a long haul.'

And of course, the major knew his army well, since we finally withdrew from the jungle after seven days. But no mincing of words: straight soldiers talk about what to expect, with a reminder that each man present was a volunteer, handpicked and the best the army had. Strikingly, there was no mention of mission success—to clear the camp; just a mention of their standing as fighting men. The SF were firm adherents of the old adage, 'Who cares who wins?' The major was simply exhorting his men to fight hard and well; the rest would follow. Well, in the true sense, it was not really a typical pep talk, but more an invocation of their identity, of pride and responsibility. Simple stuff that I guess moved men, not promises of rewards, medals or promotions.

The other incident was when we came back from Sri Lanka after a gruelling 3-year tenure. The unit had barely settled in when orders came to be on a 48-hour standby for a parachute operation on a foreign airfield. Morale plummeted and you could hear a murmur of disaffection amongst the ranks. Even the officers thought it was a bit too much and that we had more than done our bit for the old country. The butcher's bill had been high and quite a few new names had been added on the KIA (killed in action) honour board. The CO, Col PC Katoch, sensed the disquiet in the unit and called for an Officer/JCO meeting.

He started with a brief history of the battalion—over two centuries of glorious fighting across the world; two World Wars and in the second one, nearly a company was wiped out fighting German paratroopers in Italy; captured the strategically important Haji Pir Pass in PoK (Pakistan-occupied Kashmir) in 1965 when it was a parachute battalion; and so and so forth. It was an impressive record and I could feel a sense of pride in the unit's past achievements.

'This, gentlemen,' the CO summed it up, 'is our fighting performance when we were normal infantry of the line or a parachute battalion. Clearly, one can expect a lot more now that we are SF. I know it is a bit unfair to be throwing us back in the fire so soon, but then nobody said it is a fair world. A 100 per cent commitment is what I ask and as we are all a volunteer force,' and he slowly made eye contact with each man in the room, 'let me give any man who wants out of this op a chance to walk away. Needless to say, he will have to quit the unit. But nothing officially will be held against him.'

It is obvious that none of the men present in that room, or for that matter in the unit, not even fleetingly would have pondered that offer. For the time, setting and the context, it was a perfect motivational talk, since it touched upon the history of the unit and alluded subtly to the enormous burden each of us carried to uphold that name as the inheritors of this illustrious past.

Years later, in my new avatar as a corporate man, I would always waver when expected to motivate the team. The only motivation that I had learnt was to call a spade a spade and appeal to their sense of duty. Often during team appraisals, just for devilry, I would ask the question, 'Why should the company hand out a bonus for a job that you are already getting paid for, with the tacit understanding that it would be done well?' There were no yearly hikes or bonuses in the army. In my time as a captain, I was paid a paltry 350 rupees more than my contemporaries in the other arms—a 150 rupees as parachute allowance and the other 200 as hazard money. So, financial emoluments were clearly not the reason for so many of us volunteering for a hard risky life. Perhaps part of the answer lies in what Simon Sinek said, 'People don't buy what you do; they buy why you do it.'

It is a difficult concept for an average civilian to understand that you are prepared to risk your life for reasons other than power or money. The corporate world believes in a very transactional nature of motivation. In my corporate career, I often saw far too much salary/bonus given in the hope of better performance and retention of talent. My understanding is that beyond a certain threshold, any further financial emoluments are superfluous and will not in proportion produce the required output. Results and rewards must be linked and earned gradually. More money does not necessarily guarantee better productivity and higher loyalty. Needless to say, we were all volunteers. We had endured hell to wear the maroon beret because, deep down, we thought we were different and wanted to test ourselves with the best in the game. Money was the last thing on our minds. So why were these men different?

Amongst the officers in the SF, it was a motley collection of misfits, loners, romantics and adventurers. None, when they joined, had ambitions of becoming generals. The furthest they could think of was to command their own SF battalion. They were passionate about their work and took pride in it. The whole Indian Army or certainly the fighting arms, base their entire ethos towards professional endeavour in one simple Urdu word—*Izzat*. It has been passed down generations to form this intangible pillar from which perhaps emanate all the other value systems that the men are encouraged and expected to adhere to. There is no exact definition of the word in English, but it broadly encompasses a few attributes—honour, prestige, dignity, glory, respect, reputation, etc. In the Western military culture, the closest meaning would be honour.

It is a powerful word which makes all speeches redundant, and often an entire motivational talk before a battle or a task is summed up by just one word—*izzat.* Do it for your and the unit's *izzat.* Over the years, men have gone to an early grave upholding that belief in not letting down the honour of the unit. Every officer, commanding men in action, has at some stage used that word. When I passed out of the military academy and was heading up to the unit for my probation, the only thing my father, a colonel from the old school, said as he shook my hand was: 'Do not let the side down, boy. It is a question of the family's *izzat.*'

I do not think he would have fretted too much if I had failed my selection, but more importantly, he was also alluding to my conduct. Even if you go down, go down with dignity and grace. And some of the other stellar values such as honesty and integrity are also subsumed in that one word—*izzat.* I shall cover the latter in a later chapter. Often in my corporate career, when for cost-cutting reasons, the hikes and the bonuses were not to everyone's expectation and one could discern a noticeable drop in productivity and morale, I would try and bring up this word—of course, garbed in more graspable language, which appealed to their sense of duty. For I always found it difficult to impress upon the team the sense of duty that they owed to their work and so to the organisation. The concept of *izzat,* I suppose, cannot be verbalised, but must be learnt the hard way through a process.

My approach, however, was the same as it was in the SF. You

joined the company of your volition—nobody forced you—at a mutually agreed salary to perform a certain function. So, as long as you collect a salary, I need my work done. If you are so unhappy, leave. But till then, professionalism and work ethics demand that you deliver for your own reputation. Some understood and imbibed those values, and I am sure, have benefited overall, while most preferred the allure of materialistic avariciousness to define their ethics. The above is not exactly an apple-to-apple comparison, but I mention it only to bring forth the fact that life is not fair and motivation to perform should not always be coupled with success or reward.

Having said that, most folks at an early age are not fortunate enough to be clear-headed about the professional path they want to take. Others, while passionate about a career, may achieve their goal. However, longevity in the same line may come under duress due to many reasons—boredom, stress, lack of self-actualisation, etc., even compassionate reasons for that matter, especially in the army, can make continuity untenable. With many more job opportunities and a diverse selection of professions to choose from, there is a noticeable tendency for constant change, to the extent of often switching industries. Job security is no more a criterion to cling to a job and self-actualisation, it seems, has become the norm. A simple definition of self-actualisation is the process by which an individual realises his full potential by pursuing personal growth, creativity and self-fulfilment. It is the highest level in Maslow's hierarchy theory and revolves around a person's ability to live independently, without structuring their lives around other people's opinions and instructions. The quote 'what you can become, you must become' is very apt here.

There is no problem with that line of thought, except that it generally applies to more creative and independent pursuits. Try becoming a self-actualised person in an organisation, especially in the army, and it will not be long before you will be shown the exit door. This expectation today, though in a tempered form, is the bane of many a career being cut short. There is a tendency to get bored and disillusioned quickly. Often, this loss of interest in one's career or work is experienced when one is up against some major pressure or stress. A sense of entitlement is the last thing a person beginning his career should carry with him when starting a job. If you are looking at independence of action, then try your hand at creative pursuits, acting, dancing, art, etc.

Having said that, however, if you are constantly unhappy in a job or a situation in life and have given it reasonable time, you have two choices: strive to improve the situation or quit. No point dancing when the music has stopped. You are doing a disservice to yourself and the organisation. However, till you are accepting a pay cheque, you have a responsibility to deliver to the employer. And as my father often reminded me, 'Never quit a sinking ship.' It is not only bad, in the ethical sense, but also habit-forming. You will invariably be tempted to quit when the going gets tough. Always leave if you must when you are at the top. And of course, to drive home the point subtly, he would rattle off the poem 'Casabianca'—'The boy stood on the burning deck, Whence all but he had fled.'

It is a very personal value system and in certain circumstances exceedingly difficult to follow and implement in its entirety. While I had decided to quit the army at some stage, the decision about 'when' had not been taken and came about in a very unusual way. I was deployed in Kashmir and had spent two years with a newly raised Commando RR unit. Before getting posted to the valley, I had been operating with the team in the north-east, again a hard place to work. Militancy was at its peak in Kashmir in those days and the hectic pace of operations was extracting a heavy toll—both mental and physical—on the men in the field. I was out on patrol early one morning in the Lolab Valley, climbing up to the heights in forested terrain, when we came under fire. It was from across a small stream further up the mountain, just a burst or two, inaccurate and from a distance. It seemed the man was retreating uphill when he sighted us through the trees and engaged, in the confidence that we were too far to be a threat.

Everybody hit the dust as the bullets went awry, hitting the trees above our head and shredding twigs and pinecones. I raised my head and made eye contact with some of the others. Then I noticed the man behind me a little down the path. He was a JCO who had joined us recently from a peace station. It was obvious he was in a blue funk, for while everybody was up and about, this man was still prone—his head covered with his hands and buried in a mound of earth. I found it very amusing, and picking up a few small pinecones, I tossed them at him, shouting 'grenade'. His body went rigid and he dug himself deeper into the mound. Everybody cracked up.

As Murakami recalled in one of his books about how and exactly when, during a baseball game, he took the decision to quit his existing work and become a writer, I think my moment to leave the army was then. The juvenility of my behaviour suddenly struck me—mocking a senior man in a moment of danger. The humour in the situation was replaced with self-reproach. I now viewed my time in operations as childish and a dangerous game of cops and robbers. It dawned on me that the child in me was dying and so was the humour, and if that happened, frontline soldiering was going to be a miserable experience here on. I recalled reading somewhere: 'That men of action are, after all, only instruments of men of thought.' Howsoever much I loved the profession of arms, I certainly did not want to be an instrument in anyone's hand. The professional goal had shifted completely and with that, went the motivation for any further SF soldiering. However, I followed what Viktor Frankl said, 'When we are no longer able to change a situation, we are challenged to change ourselves.'

At the same time, it is in the nature of SF soldiering to believe that a good man discerns there is something wrong with the fellow who seeks jobs in the rear and is loath to become one of them. And while there is a chance of action, he must endeavour to take part in it. The prevalence of this simple conjecture impels him to volunteer for the risky jobs repeatedly. As long as there is a risky job on the horizon, he will walk towards it. Action calls and he answers—again and again—not out of bravado, but because he cannot stomach sitting it out while others bleed. It is this raw, relentless instinct that drives him to keep raising his hand for the jobs no one else wants.

This ingrained moral code was what helped me grind through the demanding times, following what a wise old Sufi saint once said, 'I went in and left myself out.' At its heart, the phrase has tremendous depth and means surrendering ego, expectation and self-interest at the door of duty. You 'go in'—into the fire, the fog, the fight—with full presence. But you leave behind your complaints, doubts, fears and desires for comfort or recognition. You act with purpose, not personal gain. It is the same code that drives a soldier to move towards gunfire while others seek cover. Sometimes in life, one needs to think: 'It is not about me right now. It is about what needs to be done.'

It is a pity that an essential moral code about developing a sense of duty is not something taught in our schools. It was a hallmark of the British public school system during the Victorian era and it was often remarked that the British empire was won on the playing fields of Eton, Harrow and Rugby. All three were the top public schools in England during that time.

But as they say, sometimes leaving the army is more difficult than joining it. From the time I put in my papers for release from service, it was another year plus before the authorities decided to post me out of Kashmir. And that was the toughest year, as you went about leading men in combat, in harsh mountain country, when all wish to do so had been replaced with the thought of a tranquil, comfortable existence.

In essence, true motivation ideally is not something you can seek from external factors. It needs a deeper connection from within. In the SF, the men did not need external clutches such as financial incentives, gallantry awards, etc. to operate, but were driven purely by a sense of identity, pride and a deep-rooted belief and commitment to uphold their own and the unit's *izzat*. This sort of internal motivation sustains high quality performance through thick and thin, while in the corporate world a sense of transactional motivation lends itself to short bursts of energy that need sustenance through more rewards constantly. Motivation, therefore, derived from an internal sense of purpose and professionalism is what leads to long-term excellence. High professional work ethics and morals help in keeping standards. Motivation, then, is less about being inspired and more about remembering who you are and why you chose a particular path.

Takeaways

- ***Motivation must be forged from within. It cannot depend on medals, praise or paycheques.*** *Once you have accepted a task—and been compensated in cash, kind or trust—it becomes your duty to deliver everything you have got.*

- ***In our world,* izzat*—honour—is not ceremonial.*** *It is earned, daily, in how you show up for your work and your word.*
- ***In SF, we live by a simple code: actions speak. excuses do not.*** *We do not wait to be pushed. We lean in. Whether in the mud, the mountains or the mess of everyday life—the job must get done. And it must be done well. Not for applause. Not for promotion. But because that is who we are.*

ATTITUDE OUTRANKS QUALIFICATION

Right man in the right place is a devastating weapon.

–US Special Forces

On a rainy chilly January morning, I reported for probation at the unit's base up in the Himachal hills. The place looked bleak and desolate since the unit was overseas in Sri Lanka for the past two years. The grass was overgrown, the barracks dilapidated, paint peeling off, roads potholed and the whole station seemed to be sighing in an atmosphere of depressive decrepitude. The adjutant, a captain recuperating from an IED injury sustained in Sri Lanka, coldly informed me that as the unit was committed in action, the bulk of my probation would be carried out in Sri Lanka. However, the decision to send me south would be taken in the next four days.

'In that time, we would know if you are commando material

or not. No point wasting everyone's time,' he quipped with a wry smile, as he weighed me up from behind his desk. 'What would you like to do?'

'Sir, some lunch would be fine. Missed my breakfast today.'

'Fuck your lunch. I am talking about a PPT (physical proficiency test) or a BPET (battle physical efficiency test),' he snapped loudly, annoyed at my stupid response.

I chose the former, being a one-mile run with an easier set of tests. He gave me half an hour to change into my PT kit and report. The probation, it seemed, had started minus the much-needed lunch. The man waiting, my probation NCO for the next four days, looked bored and disinterested and did not jump to attention on seeing an officer. With his hands cupped under his armpits for warmth, he casually inquired my age.

'Twenty-two, *ustaad*,' I muttered.

'Well, I am thirty-two and if you can keep pace with me, you will come in excellent.' With that immodest remark, he clicked his stopwatch and took off at a steady clip.

Bold statement from a man ten years your senior and I was looking forward to shattering his arrogance. I clung to his heels, like a bored dog chasing a car, nudging him from time to time, to increase the pace, by lengthening my stride. Suddenly, the road bifurcated and went up a steep hill. Briefly, he slowed and then, leaning into the incline, he surged forward powerfully and rocketed up the hill, to disappear into the gathering mist. He was waiting for me at the finish line in the same posture, hands cupped under his armpits, with not a drop of sweat on his brow or a breath out of order. Clearly, the run had not even warmed him up.

'Fail,' he said, 'in here, there is no good or fair. You are either excellent or you fail.'

Anyway, the next couple of days they kept me busy with classes and a couple of hours of vicious physical training session called commando PT. The adjutant, whenever he ran into me, was derisive to the point of being insulting, encouraging me to quit, as he could see I was not cut out for the unit. The nights he made interesting by detailing me as the duty officer, with orders to check all the sentries across the station twice at night. The last day in the unit, I opted for the 40-kilometre speed march with 60 pounds of weight—perhaps the toughest physical test in the battery of tests. The rest of the tests I reckoned could be done in Sri Lanka, provided I cleared this one. The captain, I felt by then, had taken one of those instant dislikes to me and was making no bones about his feelings. The humiliation was getting to me and it was pointless prolonging it, especially when I knew it would all come to naught.

Gruelling physicals, sleep deprivation, isolation, hectoring and the verbal torment were slowly eroding my will and my mind had started to process escape scenarios from the victimisation that I felt was blatant. Most important was how I would explain the failure to my father. After a vicious session of commando PT in the morning, at two in the afternoon, the speed march started. My probation NCO, Jai Baksh was pacing me. By then, my only aim was to finish the speed march in excellent timing and then have the satisfaction of telling the captain that having cleared their toughest test, I had no intention to stay back, thank you very much. To finally be the giver rather than a taker and to see the captain's incredulous expression would be gratification enough for all the indignity and discomfiture I had suffered. In fact, the departing speech was ready in my mind. In hindsight, I reckon the only reason I managed to clear that speed march was because of the seething anger which had been simmering within me since I had landed.

This is a good example of how anger, an extremely negative emotion, in certain circumstances, can be turned to your advantage if given concrete direction. The emotion of hate and anger is a power often used during war. The Americans in Vietnam went about motivating their men by telling them, 'Don't get sad, get even.' This stimulation of aggressive rage, if directed down a narrow path of serious passion upon some external goal or quarry, will by and large always produce concrete results.

At 30 kilometres, my pace slowed to a walk, as days of fatigue came crashing down on me like a ton of bricks. My legs felt heavy, my mind floundered and an all-consuming weariness overwhelmed me. The anger that had sustained me so far seemed to have dissipated like the day, since it had grown dark. A villager on a cycle sidled up to us and got chatting. Very kindly, he offered to carry my pack on his cycle and even offered me a ride. Jai Baksh thought it was a great idea, since my walking pace did not bode well for the timing. He urged me to take up the offer. Briefly, my weakened mind flirted with the idea, but a second sense warned me to decline. It was not unprecedented for the probation NCO to suggest a shortcut or a lift during a speed march when the candidate was mentally at his most vulnerable state. Many probationers fell for that trick and were at once shown the exit gate. Integrity is often put to test under the burgeoning strains of mental and physical pressure. I will touch upon it further down in the chapter.

Anyway, in the distance down the road, I saw the glimmering light of a storm lantern placed on the bonnet of a 3-ton truck. That tiny flickering flame, like in the fabled story of Birbal and Akbar, became my beacon of hope, the end to my suffering. I trudged on, with Jai Baksh exhorting me to dig deep and give it all. Seven minutes under the excellent timing, I staggered across the finish line. I had barely recovered my breath when the captain drove up from behind. He looks at me, checks his watch and tells me there is a bridge half a kilometre ahead, which I need to touch and be back within the cut-off time. Noticing my unbelieving expression, he leans out of the window and tells me, 'So far so good. I will catch you at the bridge. Now we will see if you are Special Forces material or not.'

The human mind is designed to work around goals and the goal I had set for myself was 40 kilometres. To achieve it, at some stage during the latter part of the run, I had latched on to the lantern light in the far distance—the end of my misery. But I guess that is not what captain *sahib* had in mind. They clearly wanted to test if I had that extra bit in me to go beyond the given task/goal. In hindsight, now I understand what he meant when he said, 'Now we will see if you are Special Forces material or not.' The real test was the extra 1 kilometre and not the 40 kilometres I had wrapped up in the given timeline.

From an evolutionary perspective, humans developed goal-oriented thinking; and motivation accordingly is deeply tied to goal setting. As per Edwin Locke and Gary Latham, specific and challenging goals significantly enhance performance and motivation compared to vague or easy goals. In other words, telling someone 'do your best' is not nearly as effective as saying 'finish this task by 5 p.m. with zero errors.' Specificity creates clarity. Challenge sparks effort. The mind, therefore, is structured to work most effectively ideally when it has defined goals to pursue. The actual test comes in when you change the goal post at the last moment. Perhaps the captain had read the theory, since that is exactly what he had in mind. He knew I had mentally latched on to a particular distance and time and upsetting it even by a trifle would test my resilience.

Anyway, I am still gawping at him as he drives off. I sway on my feet, benumbed with exhaustion and fatigue; my back has lacerations and I am in a foul mood. Enough is enough. Chucking my pack and rifle, I sit down and refuse to move. Jai Baksh now intervenes and shakes me by the shoulder, picks up the rifle and pack and starts to run. I shake off my inertia and inadvertently follow him. I take back my rifle and pack and tell him I am not interested in continuing. Jai Baksh, the old soldier, detected some redeeming quality in me that even I was not aware of. That is what a probation is supposed to do—peel off the layers and expose the hitherto shrouded sides of a man's character. Jai Baksh had not just been pacing me; he had been watching me intently all along—not for speed, but for the spirit so essential to be an SF soldier. I did not know it then, but I know now that he had been reading my will. He looks me in the eye and tells me very sternly that the worst is over and now, if I give up due to a few more minutes of discomfort, the regret of those minutes will last me a lifetime. It was the toughest kilometre I have ever run, but how true he was! Thank you, Jai Baksh *sahib*, who retired as the SM of the battalion in his time.

The fact was that I was unacquainted with the procedure and the progression of a selection process. With the unit committed in Sri Lanka, there were no other officers around to guide me. The aim is to test you not only physically but also mentally and psychologically. They could still make some compromises on the physical aspects, in the assumption that over time, amongst a body of very fit men, one would naturally come up the curve. But if an individual did not have the right attitude, nothing could be done about it. It was one of the most important attributes the SF would vet you for, an absence of which would disqualify you at once—the attitude of *never say die*.

The selection was designed to test how passionately you wanted that maroon beret, juxtaposed to how persistently the SF could deny you that privilege, in a given timeframe. Those who have gone through an SF selection will vouch for the fact that it has to be an uncompromising passion, a *junoon* (madness), a single-minded focus, with mind space for no other thought or aim, but the sole desire to be badged into the elite club. Reminds me of what Rumi said, 'I have tried caution and forethought; from now on I shall make myself mad.'

In another anecdote of sheer do-or-die attitude, I recall an officer who reported for probation, where I was detailed as his junior probation officer. On a scorching sultry day, we conducted his 20-kilometre-speed march again, timed and with sixty pounds on the back. Those were the days when few people had any idea about hydration, calories, diet, etc. for, an endurance run. You ran on water and a few oranges and other fruits that the training team bought off the nearest fruit stall. The pack you carried was World War II vintage, called the pack 08 and had the thinnest straps, which over time with the weight, bit into your shoulders cutting off the blood supply to the arms.

The probationer was making good speed when suddenly mid-distance, he staggered and collapsed. We put him in the vehicle, where he revived and insisted on continuing with the run. I refused. The next day, he was given another chance, and this time the senior probation officer, a major, was there along with us. Another sweltering day and another dismal performance, for it was a repeat of the day before. Except this time when he collapsed, he hauled himself up to his feet immediately and continued running. Then he fell a second time, got up, staggered some distance, before crumbling again. Clearly, it was a severe case of dehydration leading to cramps, because his limbs seemed to have gone numb. But then he did a bizarre thing. He started to crawl. On being told by the major to stop and get back into the vehicle, he requested permission to continue.

When we came back, I discussed with the major, mentioning he should be packed off on grounds of physical deficiency—two chances and both ending in failure. It speaks volumes of the major that despite all my remonstrance, he completely disregarded my suggestion. With his experience, he had discerned something in the man, which my untrained eyes had not seen. And I am glad to say that he did not pay any heed to my unqualified opinion, because the unit would have lost an exceptionally fine officer and the Indian Army a major general. In due course, he became one of the fittest men in the unit, that is, amongst a body of men for whom toughness is a byword.

Qualifications will get you a job, but it is the attitude that will take you up in life. That is why the US SF believed in the saying, 'The right man in the right place is a devastating weapon.' If you get that right, you get quality output because invariably you have a person who has the attitude and the aptitude for the task at hand. I labour the point mainly because, in the corporate world, I saw an almost apathetic approach by recruiters towards finding the right attitude in a potential candidate for a job. The SF believed in quality over quantity, and in my time, most SF units were running at 50 per cent of their officer strength. They refused to compromise, since they understood that selecting the right men is half the secret of success in war, as it is of most of the achievements in peace. The effect of wrong hiring can be highly detrimental to an organisation eventually. This is because mediocrity breeds mediocrity.

While I saw the damaging effect of mediocrity in the various organisations I worked for over the years, let me narrate an incident of the same from the opposition I faced in the army. It is early morning somewhere in the north Lolab Valley in Kashmir. The radio sets are running on intercept mode and I am rummaging around in my rucksack for something. The sound of a *kalma* wafts across from the radio, followed by the voice of Mike Charlie (MC). Nobody pays attention, since it is a common station which comes alive twice a day. He is the professional handler sitting on a Pakistani post, probably Lohsar-1, who handles taking an attendance roll call of all the *jehadi* stations active in the Lolab and Rajwar areas. He runs rapidly through the numerous radio call signs, Sheshwar, Triple one, Sher Khan and so on, with someone from time to time reporting in with the usual *salaam-alaikum* and *all ok*, or with the latest sitrep (situation report), or perhaps a request for something which needs to be addressed.

A lively Kashmiri voice tunes in and starts to give a very elaborate sitrep. It draws my attention because he is talking about an operation I was involved in. Well, it was hardly an operation, as I had dropped into Shumrial village randomly, on my way back from the divisional HQ, to chat up an informer. Somebody engaged us from the forested hills around, and after a brief exchange of fire, everything quietened down. The militant on the radio was clearly the perpetrator, since other than claiming he had engaged us, the man went off on a rampage of exaggerated storytelling. He narrated how the entire village was cordoned off by the dogs (security forces) and how a handful of militants took on the opposition, which was in much greater numbers.

Now I would not have intervened if he had limited himself to engaging larger numbers. Perhaps while reporting, a bit of imaginative heroics is permissible if you need to climb up the *jehadi* career, but I was certainly not going to allow him to get away with blatant lies of how huge numbers of casualties were inflicted on us and finally the choppers came in to ferry the wounded away. Warming up to his tale, he had just reached the point where he and his team were engaging the choppers, when I butted in politely with the usual salutations to Allah.

'MC,' I said, 'the man is lying through his teeth. He just fired off a burst or two and then legged it up the hill. I am the man who was on the ground. No firefight, no casualties, no choppers, zilch—all a figment of his imagination. If you have any authority, I recommend you sack him since, if Jehad-e-Kashmir must continue and freedom from the infidels is the goal, then you need ethical upright men of integrity.'

I thought MC would be appreciative of my candid feedback on one of his local commanders and thank me; instead, to my complete surprise, he turned on me.

'Mind your business, *fauji bhai*,' he snapped at me. 'You guys do the same in the army. False, exaggerated reports are often sent up the chain to get medals and promotions. So do not preach me on morality and honourable conduct. Now, I suggest you leave the channel and let me finish with my reporting.'

The above needs no explanation. The so-called line manager MC, clearly a mediocre *jehadi* sitting comfortably in a Pakistani post, is accepting a falsified report without questioning from an equally mediocre, unmotivated senior local *mujahid* in the field. The consequence was a noticeable drop in contacts and engagements with us, other than giving the army an upper hand to dominate the area. Not surprisingly, the man on the ground was sacked shortly and a more focused battle-hardened Paki commander made his entry to revive the lost momentum. Lord Moran, in his study of men in combat, made a pertinent point: 'That men of character in peace will invariably be men of courage in war.' Both these gentlemen were clearly unprincipled men, and if there were more like them in the higher echelons of the *jehadi* command, then fortunately for us, it did not augur well for the future of *jehad* in Kashmir.

The US Army white paper on the profession of arms mentions social trust and how a professional earns the trust of their clients through their ethics, which also becomes a means of motivation and self-control. It is characterised by *cedat emptor,* let the taker believe in us. That is why in any SF probation, a very alert ear was kept open to detect the existence or signs of moral turpitude in the candidate. The slightest inclination to lie, cheat or misreport was viewed seriously and was ground enough for disqualification. Integrity and trust can only be implicit and not limited. A character bereft of any of the required virtues will significantly result in a dented attitude. The chink in the armour will be visible and the person will start to come apart under duress. I believe a person can never have a winning attitude without a set of professional ethics to achieve the same.

The personal experience of an SF selection, and then my time with them, only reinforced my belief that attitude consistently outweighs qualification when it comes to high performing teams. SF is the best example where small teams deliver big impact. Notwithstanding the importance of skill and experience, integrity, resilience and ethics are the factors that often set individuals apart. Look beyond résumés and accolades when hiring. Evaluate character, cultural fit and mindset. Go beyond finding the best candidate on paper.

Takeaways

- ***When the going gets tough, the tough do not just get going—they get leading.*** *That is what SF selection teaches you. It is not about who is the fastest or strongest. It is about who keeps moving when everything hurts.*

- ***Grit and passion often outlast brute strength****. It is not about having more muscle—it is about having more will.*
- ***In life, passion is the edge****. Without it, you perish.*
- ***Qualifications may get you through the door****. But it is your attitude that earns respect, command and legacy.*
- ***Hire for hunger, not just what's on the résumé.*** *Résumés can lie. Mindset never does.*
- ***Pressure does not just break people.*** *It reveals them.*
- ***Mediocrity begets mediocrity.*** *But integrity and trust raise the bar and build confidence in your employer/client.*

HARKAT—FIGHT INERTIA AND KEEP MOVING

When I am rolling, I exist. When I rest, I am no more.

–Muhammad Iqbal

Often, when some of us old friends who served together in the SF meet up or chat on a call, somewhere along in the conversation, the word *harkat* will pop up as a question. *Harkat* is an oft-used typical Indian Army word, literally translated to mean movement or activity. For us, however, it came to represent not only physical exertion but also the pursuit of learning, professional growth and personal advancement. Now, if the answer is a casual 'oh nothing much,' or 'all good, life goes on,' then you were in for a mouthful. This is because it instantly hints at inertia, a condition unacceptable to the group. It was inconceivable that an individual was doing nothing, regardless of whether he may be content and happy in the state. To linger in stillness was not comprehensible.

This predilection for constant *harkat* or activity became the driving mantra—to move or lose.

A negative response, for example, if one were having a rough patch in his marriage and heading towards a divorce, would be reciprocated with a simple pat on the back and a few mutterings of sympathy. But overall, the situation was considered way better than someone complaining about being bogged down in a stale relationship, incapacitated to make a decision. Relationship going south, no worry, you tried your best, did not work, now take a hard call soonest and get back on track. As the French say, '*tout casse, tout passe, tout lasse*' (everything passes, perishes and palls). In sum, nothing lasts. How the word *harkat* came about to express the general situation in life is shrouded in some uncertainty. But my understanding is that it originated in our parlance from the basic teaching the army imparts for action to be taken when under fire. The expected response is to manoeuvre from cover to cover to unsettle the enemy, overcoming the natural human instinct for self-preservation.

Latch on to concrete images, if you can, of a scenario where you are the aggressor and engage the opposition coming towards you. Case one—where he hits the ground and sticks behind cover, conveying to you the opposition's inexperience and fear. It will encourage you to close the distance and annihilate him. Case two—analogous situation, but this time you glimpse movement. Bodies are moving from rock to rock, in what the army manuals instruct as the 'one leg on the ground', the fire and move principle. In that moment, the significance of constant action becomes undeniable. And if the contact is close enough, you hear commands being shouted. Well, it is disconcerting and the respect for the opposition goes up at once. You wonder what he is up to and are concerned that he may encircle you. Either way, the message is clear: he is going to give you a fight. It certainly had me worried once in Sri Lanka, where in a jungle firefight I could hear the Tiger commander exhorting his men in Tamil to hedge us in from an exposed front. The experience further reinforced the unyielding need to keep moving. Move or die.

Any trained MMA fighter will tell you that fighting is the art of perpetual motion. Anyway, the point I make is that action, whether in work or personal life, especially in trying times, creates a sense of achievement. It reinforces the belief in yourself and boosts your self-esteem and confidence to handle tough challenges. I am simply drawing a correlation between physical movement and constructive action—a lesson I learned the hard way when under fire. Again, having served in the army and SF, I am aware that most of my examples are biased towards physical activity. But then so was the profession where my youth was spent, and therefore, all my experiences and learnings stem from an element of physicality that the profession involved.

Inertia, both mental and physical, is by far the greatest obstacle to progress. However, it also is obvious that no man can stay motivated to perform at peak all the time. Lethargy, sloth or inertia afflicts all of us from time to time. I recall an incident which brings out succinctly how the SF addressed this human frailty.

The unit was back to base from Sri Lanka after a 3-year stint. The suffering and loss of human life had been immense. The long absence was felt more heavily by the married men, especially those who had young children. Mothers were reintroducing the fathers to the kids, who in some cases had resorted to calling these bearded sunburnt men uncle. In my naïveté, I was imagining a hiatus from the usual hectic training schedule followed in an SF battalion. The case, for a week or two of free time, was compelling and nobody deserved it more than these men.

It, therefore, came as a shock to me when we were told to report for PT parade on the third day, with orders to work out our training schedule for the month. Everything was back to normal, as if the troublesome times in Sri Lanka were a figment of our imagination. I wrapped up an unenthusiastic run and sauntered up to my senior subaltern to vent out my feelings. He heard me patiently crib about the suddenness and injustice of punishing us now, after what we had gone through, and then, giving me a wary look, interjected with something that has stayed with me my whole life.

'In here,' he said, 'there is a saying: bamboo, bamboo in the grass, why ain't you up my arse? The only way,' he continued, 'to remain sharp and on top of your game is to keep using that bamboo.'

A coarse soldiering expression, but the truism of the statement cannot be doubted. In other words, put yourself in situations where the possibility of retiring or disengagement is non-existent and the only exit or escape is to commit to concrete positive action. This notion of relentless motion finds a surprising parallel in everyday life. Consider, for instance, how even the Japanese fishing industry confronted stagnation by transforming its practices to keep the catch lively and fresh by introducing a 'shark in the tank.' The anecdote goes that the Japanese, who love their fish, started to complain about the freshness of the catch. The customers complained that, as the trawlers were out for days in the sea and the catch was stored in ice, the fish was stale by the time it hit the shelves. Withering sales needed a fresh approach to storage, and so the fishing industry produced the idea to have water tanks on the ships, to ensure live fish till port.

However, in no time the finicky Japanese consumer, fish connoisseurs to a man, came back complaining that while the fish were alive and therefore fresh till the last mile delivery, the fact that they were packed tight and sat motionless in the tanks affected the taste of the fish. The fishing industry promptly went back to the drawing board. The solution they figured out was to ensure the fish got sufficient exercise to keep the suppleness of muscle so desired by the discerning consumer. Consequently, a small shark was introduced into each tank. In much the same way, an unrelated industry in the quest for fresh fish, reimagined their strategy and by introducing a small shark managed to ensure constant movement. Now, if you find your will flailing from time to time, hesitate not to introduce your personal shark in your tank. Both examples purport to the same objective: apathy is a universal malady and to defend against it, sometimes one must contrive to orchestrate an inexorable situation. Once it is *fait accompli*, you can either fail or succeed entirely. Either way, you have managed to generate *harkat* in life.

The master performers in various domains understand this concept of creating an exacting situation to extract the best out of themselves very well. The principle of creating challenges from within is not confined to physical endeavours alone. In this example, it would be more proper to call the person a grandmaster, since it is believed that in the world chess championships in the 1990s, the then world champion, Grandmaster Gary Kasparov, did exactly that. Knowing that he performed at his best in adverse conditions, and realising that the opponent was not putting him under any undue pressure, he decided to create his own stressor by going in for what subsequently came to be called in chess parlance a 'queen's gambit.' He sacrificed his queen early, a huge loss as you will agree if you have played chess, and then went on to win the game. This is a perfect parallel to the bamboo or the shark in the tank examples mentioned above, which involves creating an unrelenting, untenable position for yourself, which in turn needs a big positive response from you for a better outcome. The exception in Kasparov's case was that it was a purely mental situation on a chessboard. The consistent thread in all the above examples is clear: without perpetual motion, naturally or self-created, we run the risk of succumbing to inertia, and sometimes, like Kasparov, one must contrive a situation of discomfort to force progress. This philosophy transcends the battlefield and applies equally well to leading a dynamic, evolving personal and professional life. As the Roman philosopher-emperor Marcus Aurelius believed, 'The impediment to action advances action. What stands in the way becomes the way.' This saying inspired the Stoic phrase 'The obstacle is the way.'

As the Stoic philosophers further believed, 'There were two elements in the universe from which all things were derived, namely cause and matter. Matter lies inert and inactive, a substance with unlimited potential, but destined to remain idle if no one sets it in motion. And it is the cause (reason) which turns matter to whatever end it wishes.' Now, while I impress upon the importance of constant movement to achieve any sort of accomplishment, it is not going to happen unless one has a reason, as the Stoics believed. The existence of a goal, aim or cause is necessary for any action to be started in the first place. So, find the cause and go to work on the matter. The rest will follow. Viktor Frankl puts it across differently when he says, 'Between stimulus and response, there is space. In that space is our power. In our response lies our growth and our freedom.' Basically, one needs a stimulus. Something happens—a challenge, an event or even a thought. This is the trigger. The response is how we react—emotionally, physically, etc. The space is the critical pause between the two—at times so small that we run the risk of missing it. And in that space lies our power to choose, to respond with intent rather than impulse.

The men in the SF could not understand indecisiveness and inactivity, passionately believing in what Viktor Frankl said, 'The existential vacuum manifests itself mainly in a state of boredom.' And boredom over a period is soul-killing, smothering initiative and growth. Inevitably, boredom also subsumes a desire for change, provided you turn the state of discontentment into something constructive. One needs to understand that it is the man himself and not the life he is leading that is to be faulted. Perpetual motion, physical and mental, was not a taught skill. It was a mindset, borne out of the SF environment. It was not something that was intrinsically taught to us in the SF, but was more a by-product that often comes about when a motley cast of unusual people are thrown together. In time, it ingrains into the inherently combative, competitive alpha male culture. They were a bunch of restless doers, and any protracted period of inactivity, especially involving lack of physical or exhilarating and risky action, led them to start questioning their raison-d'être in life. They had, as the Germans say, 'torschlusspanik,' a word that does not exist in any other language (literally translates as 'gate-closing panic', referring to the feeling that the 'gate' of opportunity is closing and time is running out). Inertia, as I said before, is by far the greatest threat to progress. Let me narrate an incident of how boredom manifests itself in a body of healthy, fit young men, living in the back of beyond with no opportunities for letting off steam. Boredom can be either a curse or a cure for inertia.

A team of ours landed up in a place called Masimpur in the Cachhar hills in Assam for trans-border operations. Typical of the army, when they wanted us, it was all op immediate and once we had reported, the corps HQ promptly forgot us. We were camped in barracks, which are at the edge of a brown muddy river in the most atrocious muggy weather, waiting for some action. Within a few days, the ennui became a cause of concern, and a vigorous physical training regimen did not do much to enliven the mood.

A couple of navigation exercises in the dense tropical jungle around saw us mauled by tiger leeches, who went vigorously for anything on two legs. A jungle fire lane was improvised next and that kept us engaged for a while. Some read Kahlil Gibran and some learnt Urdu. But nothing we tried could substitute for the thrill of pure action. So, on a whim, it was decided by the four officers, all in their twenties, that if the higher authorities were not going to provide the excitement, then we would seek our own adrenaline rush. The evening saw us leaning over a British-era old arched stone bridge over the Barak river. From the highest point, it was a clean 50 feet drop to the thick, muddy swirling water below. The plan was to jump into the river and then swim to one of the banks. One look at the raging river below and the team commander promptly handed over the baton of command to me.

'Right,' said Major Bhalla, addressing me. 'Not really my specialisation, I am a combat free-faller. You are the diver, take charge. If you say go, we go.'

I looked down into the river in all earnestness and realised it was an ugly, uninviting, malevolent river with a strong current, like most rivers are in the north-east, especially post-monsoon, when they are bloated. The jump was not intimidating, since all of us were paratroopers; it was the uncertain perils that awaited us once we hit the water. My fear was that we might not be able to negotiate the current and end up being washed up in Bangladesh. Courage faltered, or at the point of action, the syndrome of paralysis by analysis set in. Once you dither, especially in ventures where risk to life or injury is possible, the probability is 50:50 of your going through with it. A dispirited bunch returned, determined to seek out some other form of excitement to assuage our dented ego and pride.

The next plan was even more ambitious. At our riverside camp near Silchar, a narrow, meter-gauge train would trundle past daily, crossing the bridge right next to us. The plan we cooked up was absurd on the face of it, but we hoped to execute it with military precision. We would buy tickets, board the train like ordinary passengers and at the exact moment it crossed the bridge over the muddy river, we would leap—two at a time—off the train and straight into the water. The jump itself was risky. If your timing was even slightly off, you could hit the stone abutments of the bridge on the way down. But we had been swimming in that river, knew the current and were confident.

Now, why do I mention this?

Not to glorify recklessness, but to underline a simple truth: in the absence of purpose, the human spirit will invent its own challenges. Amongst young men trained for intensity, stillness can become suffocating. So, we manufactured movement. We created danger, not for the thrill alone, but to feel alive, to beat back the creeping boredom that can rot a man from the inside out.

Was it dangerous? Absolutely. Foolish? Some would say so. But it was also a release valve—a way to remind ourselves we still had control, courage and camaraderie. Because the truth is: inertia kills more men than fear ever will.

Every person, however, is different and must figure out how to capitalise this phase of existential vacuum. All my books were a product of this state of ennui; so were a few ultramarathons and long runs. The two years of the COVID-19 phase are a perfect example of a global existential dilemma for most of us. The smarter lot promptly utilised this enforced free time for something useful and constructive. Some cooked, worked on their weight, wrote, read and attempted any number of other things they were interested in but had never got the time before, while the bulk just squandered away the opportunity, with quite a few complaining of depression and anxiety.

There is a saying that has stayed with me: 'The average human is a conformist and will herd together, stoically taking the upheavals of life, like cattle during rain.' Harsh? Perhaps. But when I look around, especially at the Gen Z generation, I see some uncomfortable truths staring back. This is not about the death-defying risks of soldiering or extreme adventure. I am talking about the everyday risks—those subtle but defining leaps we must take in our personal and professional lives: starting something new without a safety net and owning your failures instead of outsourcing them. Raised in a digital cocoon, surrounded by curated perfection on screens, too many grow up elsewhere—mentally removed from reality, physically disengaged and often spiritually disoriented. The raw, unfiltered experiences of playground brawls, scraped knees and getting lost, only to find your way back—those formative rites of passage—have been replaced by swipeable stimulation and dopamine on demand.

Often, people, especially the young, talk of boredom these days, with a confession that they did not have the faintest clue how to address it. The pervasive boredom reveals an inability to address the void. So much time is frittered away in this state that some seem to be suffering from mild depression—a pattern rooted in a fear of commitment and a mind bereft of curiosity. People shy away from committing because of a fear of the result. The trend is visible in their relationships too. They follow a simple principle—if you do not try, you do not fail and your ego and pride remain unscathed. It is easy to dwell in the realms of assured conjecture, that of course they would have achieved their goal had they just tried. This living in denial and shying away from commitment, for fear of losing, is a great disservice to the self. An ultra-runner very aptly summed this up, 'Ever tried. Ever failed. No worry. Try again, fail again. Fail better.' This is beautifully summed up, reminding us that success lies in taking risks, even if failure is inevitable.

What is the result of this? A creeping conformity, a fear of discomfort and an unwillingness to commit fully to anything. And when things do not go their way, a fragile sense of identity shatters too easily. But let me be clear: this is not to dismiss an entire generation as losers. Far from it. In fact, I have seen flashes of brilliance—young minds with staggering IQs and remarkably evolved emotional intelligence. Some are fearless creators, disruptors and thinkers, raising the bar for what humans can do. And when they decide to go all in, they do so with fire and focus. The problem is not a lack of potential. It is a lack of confrontation—with the self, with hardship, with reality. What this generation needs is not more comfort, but more clarity. Not more entitlement, but exposure—to struggle, failure, consequence and ultimately, to their own strength.

There is a well-researched phenomenon more commonly referred to as 'comfort creep'. It is a psychological tendency in which a person's baseline of what he or she considers 'comfortable' gradually increases over time. As new comforts are introduced in life and become the new normal, existing older levels of comfort become unacceptable, leading to a perpetual pursuit of more ease. The key message is that humans constantly move their comfort goalposts. Take, for example, air conditioners at home or in the car: a luxury once upon a time, they are now a standard expectation, making life without them a hardship.

Biologically, humans have evolved in environments that require physical exertion, exposure to the elements, and, occasionally, hunger. Modern comfortable living creates a mismatch with our biology, which, as mentioned, ideally requires a certain level of stress, implying that small, beneficial doses of discomfort are necessary for optimal health and resilience. Constant pursuit of evolving comfort has been linked to potential long-term mental and physical issues. People who routinely seek out discomfort tend to be more motivated and engaged. If anything, it is worth following what a famous British general, Orde Wingate of the Chindits fame during WWII, is believed to have once said, 'A person must, from time to time, undergo severe physical punishment and privations, so as to enjoy the comforts of civilisation.' Easier said than done, you would say.

The good news is that willpower is not born, it is built. Grit can be trained. Risk-taking is a muscle. And the moment we stop shielding young people from difficulty and start demanding more of them, they rise. They always do.

I believe even the smallest of endeavours entails the need for a certain amount of physical or mental action, opposed by equally compelling reasons for not trying it. In my talks,

I often illustrate this with a simple example. If asked to move from the front row to the back now, the mind will quickly conjure many excuses—comfort in the familiar, the proximity to the speaker or just the inertia to stay put—all legitimate reasons for avoiding the move. Imagine then: if the endeavour was more significant, causing one to quit their comfort zones drastically, how vehemently will the mind resist a commitment to action? Discomfort is, therefore, directly proportional to the immensity and size of the goal. The bigger your goal, the more the discomfort and greater the need for commitment and consistency. Having covered the transforming power of physical or mental action to combat inertia, let me briefly touch upon the other three C's, i.e., curiosity, commitment and consistency, which form the core values, or character traits, of an average SF operator.

Aristotle believed that the ancient Greeks were superior men, since they had a mind for inquiry. A curious mind will rarely be plagued by boredom, as it will constantly seek interests and hobbies. Aristotle's most famous student was Alexander and none can deny his curiosity for the unknown world—one of the reasons which compelled him to keep advancing to the next unexplored horizon ahead. The British SF, the famous SAS (Special Air Service) disseminated amongst its men a couplet which decidedly exemplifies the ethos of remaining curious as an SF operator. It is also one of my favourite quotes from the poem 'The Golden Journey to Samarkand' by James Elroy Flecker.

We are the Pilgrims, master; we shall go

Always a little further; it may be

Beyond the last blue mountain barred with snow

Across that angry or that glimmering sea.

These lines, taken from Flecker's poem about the ancient Silk Road and the mythical city of Samarkand, are not just about geography—they are about a mindset. The journey is not undertaken for trade or riches, but for something deeper: a hunger to push past known limits, to seek what lies beyond the edge of certainty. It is a line of thought that resonates powerfully with those in the SF. In the SF, we were not chasing gold or glory—we were chasing excellence. And like the pilgrims in the poem, we kept going 'a little further,' because we understood this truth early: boredom breeds weakness; inconsistency corrodes discipline; and failure often comes disguised as comfort.

The dread of failure was real—but it was not paralysing. It was fuel. It made us show up every day, come hell or high water and train like our lives depended on it—because often, they did. And our training was not shallow. It was brutal. It was realistic and sometimes dangerous to life. You did not just learn—you learned fast. As the saying goes, 'Nothing makes you learn quicker and appreciate a teacher more than running the risk of getting shot by him'. This is because sometimes the man teaching you would be the one firing live rounds over your head.

The profession demanded craftsmanship over showmanship. It called for unshakeable commitment and consistency—the kind you cannot fake and no one else can do for you. Like the pilgrims, we journeyed not for applause, but for purpose—always a little further, always forward. This was because the risk of failure is related to the consistent effort and diligence you put into the preparation for the task at hand. Mock drills and rehearsals are carried out repetitively before any operation, and any mistakes, lacunae in planning or any omission in the conduct of the operation is addressed threadbare to mitigate the risk of failure. Failure during training was acceptable and good, since it gave you a chance to take corrective action, embodying the Japanese concept of Wabi-sabi—to embrace imperfection instead of stressing and quitting in expectation of a quick result. To take any action is better than no action at all. And once committed, no endeavour is going to see the light of day unless there is consistency. Inconsistency, it seems, is the only thing in which men are consistent. To paraphrase Denzel Washington, 'Without commitment, you will never start, and without consistency, you will never finish…fall down five times and get up six times.'

The dread of failure, as I mentioned above, deters a lot of people from ever reaching their full potential. Perhaps we need to learn from nature, which understands the concept of failure and is not averse to it. The Law of Wastage, as it unfolds in the natural world, presupposes a certain amount of loss to the environment and factors for it accordingly. For example, trees giving out seeds will see most of them eaten by birds; out of three bear cubs, two will die in infancy. And a hunting lion pride has a success ratio of only about 30-40 per cent. None of these failures or losses deters nature from abandoning their efforts. It is only humans who have an expectation of constant success, and most of the time, a quick return on the effort. Commitment and consistency in anything comes to naught if you allow despondent thoughts of failure to creep into your mind: 'Dream big, start small, but most of all, start.'

Having said that, any plan or endeavour, therefore, must have a built-in plan B for any contingency. Mental and physical preparedness is half the battle. I recall raising this point in a corporate talk, where the organisation was gearing up for exponential growth. While the business plan had been signed up and recruitment was progressing, I drew the attention of the senior and middle management to the long hours of work, constant travel and the overall heightened prolonged stress that was in the offing. Were they and their families as a group prepared to go through the grind and the discomfort the plan entailed? Because if you are not, resolution will waver and attrition of staff is a guaranteed consequence. The ability to predict problems, especially disruptions, applies to life too and nothing unexpected should rattle you enough to offset the normal balance of life. Seneca summed it well: 'Do not give in to adversity, never trust prosperity and always take full note of fortune's habit of behaving just as she pleases. Whatever you have been expecting for some time comes as less of a shock.' Remind yourself often that neither success nor failure should completely sway you and the focus should be on being mentally and physically robust.

'Nothing,' as the saying goes, 'is either good or bad, only the mind makes it so.' Mental and physical robustness was a necessary trait if one had to survive in the army, especially in the SF. The existence of the above qualities gave one the ability to adapt with agility to different terrains, weather and ever-changing combat situations—the ability to adapt to disruption. My suggestion to the young just starting off in their professional life is to travel light, both physically and mentally. Attachments to people and places hamper mobility and consequently growth. That is not to say that one should not have relationships and attachments, just get a grip over those emotions which have the potential to bind you down. Be nimble and go where opportunity demands. In my three-and-a-half years in Kashmir, I must have moved locations over twenty times. And by this, I refer to moves where I stayed put for a minimum of a month. Sri Lanka was another such whirlwind tour. The choppers would pick us up every other day and drop us wherever an infantry battalion had been mauled, a LTTE camp had to be busted or there was need for area domination. In jocularity, we used to call ourselves the whores of the army. Anybody could take us anytime.

It is not easy to be living off a rucksack and a trunk and jumping locations like a monkey on a tree, and that too in a combat environment. Ask any army officer with twenty years of service and he will tell you the number of postings he has had, with or without his family. This kind of relocation is not easy to handle unless the mind and body are trained and prepared for disruption. While I have no data to support, I do recall, however, reading somewhere the extraordinary success and achievements in the corporate and other civilian professions of *fauji* kids, as they are called in the defence services. Following their fathers from posting to posting, making friends in every new school and the overall exposure that comes with travelling gives one qualities of adaptability, mental resilience and social skills. This is a great advantage when one must follow opportunities later in life. The ones I met in the corporate world were always very polite, affable and good at their work.

Years ago, I authored some articles for a magazine under the heading 'The Diary of a Special Forces Officer.' In one of the articles, I mentioned about the dizzying speed of our professional life. I recall a phase where I had gone across to Agra for my annual refresher jumps, which included two days and a night jump in full battle gear. Five days later, I returned to the unit up in the hills and was told to get a diving team ready quickly, for a bus full of people had fallen into a canal near Kurukshetra and the civilian authorities had asked for divers. Off I went, and seeing the heart-wrenching scene at the spot, began diving at once to retrieve the bodies. It was January and we had no wetsuits for cold water diving. Four days later, I came back to the unit to find the place deserted. I was told the unit had moved off to Churdhar, a 4-hour drive further up, to conduct their mountain warfare training. The

CO had left instructions for me to join up at once. A rations truck was heading that way, so I hopped in with my rucksack. A day later, I was trudging up the mountain at 9,000 feet with the rest of my team. As I sat on a promontory, munching on a dry *puri* and shivering, I recall thinking to myself, 'Man! this is some speed. In twelve days, I had jumped out of an aircraft, dived in some canal and now I was sitting atop a mountain.' The experiences and the constant movement in the SF taught me to remain nimble and helped me in the early years of my life in the corporate world, and was one of the reasons that I was prepared to relocate to any city, provided the money and the responsibility were good enough.

While job security was sought after in my time, self-actualisation, as mentioned in an earlier chapter has become the norm now, with the new generation switching a few industries/professions as an accepted practice. Adaptability, therefore, becomes even more important if one is going to make such enormous adjustments with jobs, places, bosses and so on. It was Heraclitus, I think, who made the saying quite common in usage today, 'Change is the only constant.' How true, and only by adapting and accepting change will one alleviate the tribulations and travails in the path of life.

As mentioned in Chapter 3, one practice I followed during annual goal-setting sessions was simple but deliberate. After we discussed professional targets, I would ask each team member to commit to one personal goal—something they had been meaning to do but kept putting off: run a half-marathon;

start a blog; buy that first house. It did not matter what it was—as long as it mattered to them. Come appraisal time, I would revisit it. It was my small way of nudging them to look beyond the routines of daily work and life, to spark a little interest, a little movement, beyond the mundane. Sometimes, all someone needs is a little permission to dream again.

And while you are setting yourself goals, both in your profession and your personal life, do not shy away from pushing the envelope. You do not really know what you can get away with until you give it a shot. This was one of the first things I learnt as I went through the SF probation. So many years down the line and I am still amazed as to how I managed to scrape through selection and the many other tough times thereafter. Guess I would not have ever known if I had not pushed the bar and tried. SF encouraged a culture of pushing the limits and not just physically. The informal understanding was that if you have not been explicitly told a *No* to do something, then you could safely assume it as a *Yes* and give it a try. This was more acceptable and specifically encouraged, especially in combat scenarios. As the expression goes, 'It is easier to get forgiveness than permission.'

Ultimately in a nutshell, a successful life and career requires *harkat*. To be nimble, adapt with agility and keep pushing against all odds. Whether in the SF or in a corporate boardroom or in your personal life, set goals, commit, persist through failure and it would be a life well lived, distinguished from one mired in inertia. Personally, I am an adherent to something I read years ago, 'The active man should be able to take things easily, while the man who is inclined towards repose should, when necessary, be capable of vigorous action.' To this, I would add the capability for pursuing mental and intellectual ventures too.

Takeaways

- ***Stay in* harkat*. Stay alive.*** *Motion is life. Whether physical, mental or spiritual—keep moving. Stagnation rusts the soul.*
- ***Inertia is the silent killer of progress.*** *It creeps in quietly and settles deep. Overcome it with momentum—small daily action beats grand intentions left undone.*
- ***Boredom is a spark—if you know how to use it.*** *Left unchecked, it leads to numbness, but channelled right, boredom breeds ideas, reinvention and a hunger to create.*
- ***Do not dodge commitments for fear of failing.*** *Goals require showing up—even on the hard days. Commitment without consistency is just noise.*
- ***Conformity is comfortable, but dangerous.*** *The herd feels safe, but it is where originality goes to die. Don't be afraid to think differently—even if you walk alone.*
- ***Take risks—calculated ones.*** *Risks fuel growth. Prepare. Train. Study. And then step forward. You do not need to be reckless to be brave.*
- ***Big goals demand big discomfort.*** *If your ambition does not scare or stretch you, it is not big enough. Discomfort is not a sign of failure—it is proof you are growing.*

- ***Comfort produces fragile performers.*** *One of the biggest threats to performance is often excess comfort. When people are protected from pressure, consequence and failure, they look competent until conditions turn hostile. Then they break. The Special Forces don't train for comfort.*
- ***Embrace pressure—avoidance is toxic.*** *Discomfort is how capability is revealed and leaders emerge. Individuals/teams that cannot function under pressure will struggle or come apart under extreme duress.*
- ***Enjoy the journey—that is where life happens.*** *As a lot of wise people remind us: it is not about the destination. Find joy in the process and you will carry the weight of challenge with far greater ease.*
- ***Always have a plan b****. Life does not always cooperate. Contingency is not cowardice—it is clarity under pressure.*
- ***Push the envelope. Break your own ceilings****. Innovation lives outside your comfort zone. Test your limits. Rethink the obvious. Greatness rarely looks like routine.*
- ***Build mental and physical toughness.*** *Resilience is not gifted—it is trained. Adaptability is your edge in a world that refuses to stand still.*
- ***Travel light—in luggage and in life****. Let go of what you do not need: baggage, clutter, grudges. The lightest travellers often go the furthest.*
- ***Stay curious. Play. Explore****. Be interested. Pursue hobbies that stretch and soothe you. Curiosity is fuel—and medicine.*

STAND STILL AND SALUTE

'A gift for a gift,' said Kamal straight; 'A limb for the risk of a limb.'
'Thy father has sent his son to me, I'll send my son to him!'
–*The Ballad of East and West* (Rudyard Kipling)

I was not too sure if I should insert a chapter on such a 'mundane, run-of-the-mill' subject, such as gratitude, since it is a quality widely accepted as a noble virtue to have. And enough has been said and written about it by wiser people than yours truly. But then on second thoughts, it struck me that as a combat soldier, my experiences made me acutely more conscious of always being thankful for what I have. After all, when you have seen better men than you go to their graves early, it makes you reflect on the fleeting nature and uncertainties of life. In other words, I am only plain grateful to have come this far in one piece. To have loved, lost and loved again; to have tested yourself in combat, discovering with relief that one was not a coward; the pride and privilege of serving with the most elite; to have climbed, dived and jumped out of an aircraft; the ultra-runs and the delight of skiing down a piste slope on a glorious sunny day; and to have read and written. Oh! There are so many things for which one cannot thank the giver enough.

For the larger populace, however, I had naively assumed the Covid crisis would be a great leveller, manifesting the paramountcy of time and an appreciation for the smaller things of life. But it seems human memory, in its fallibility, tends to very quickly forget tough times, extracting no lessons from the experience. Do what you have to do, when you have to do it, since time is not waiting for anyone unless it is the pyramids. Often, you run into people who will tell you they are planning to do something they love but have postponed it for a more appropriate time in the future. And that time often never arrives. However, if something is important to you, you can always find time. It just means more sacrifice and effort.

Now, gratitude can be for the life you have, acknowledging the fact that one cannot get everything, for a look around will make plain the considerable number of folks out there struggling to make a living or just victims of great misfortune. The other is the gratitude one expresses towards someone whose kindness or help you have been a recipient of. Let me narrate two incidents that bring out the latter form of gratitude—gratitude that comes from realisation that it could easily have been you in the other man's predicament or suffering.

Many moons ago, when I was a young man in college, I was up on a mountain in the final push to summit a peak during my advance mountaineering course with NIM (Nehru Institute of Mountaineering). It was an acclimatisation climb, and as I trudged up a 60-degree snow chute, from the base camp at 14,000 feet to our advance base camp at 17,000 feet, I paused every few steps, leaning on my ice axe, to regain my breath. My head was imploding and the whole exercise of climbing seemed pointless in my miserable state. Halfway through the climb, I was in my usual position, body bent over the ice axe, gulping air like a fish out of water, when a sherpa porter caught up with me. He paused and gave me a concerned look. I noticed he was carrying a 65-pounder tent and a crate full of rations—easily around 50 to 60 kg. He was wearing worn-out boots, which we in the army called the ammo boots in the old days. One of the boots had a gash in the toe, for he had crudely tied a string around it to keep it together. Snow had collected inside and he shook it as he leaned his weight against the slope to take a breather.

'Don't keep looking up to the crest line, waiting for the gradient to ease off,' he tells me, 'One small, measured step at a time. Come, follow me.'

We hit the pass and he loosened his head strap, releasing his enormous load with a sigh of relief.

'My second load ferry for the day,' he said, smiling.

I was promptly sprawled, hedged between some rocks, completely wasted and wondering at this man's strength. It was my first exposure to strong men and to the sherpas in general. He was practically carrying his own weight. I pulled out my packed lunch and spread it on a rock. A couple of frozen hard-boiled eggs, sandwiches, juice and sweets. The standard menu provided by the institute when carrying a packed meal.

'Here, Dai (brother),' I said, 'all yours. You have earned it and I seem to have lost my appetite.'

He eyed the food longingly, but refused politely.

'You need to eat,' he answered, 'you cannot climb if you do not put in food. But if you share my meal, then perhaps I can accept your kind offer.'

'Sure.'

From his patched-up woollen jacket pocket, he pulled out a package wrapped in newspaper. It had a couple of thick coarse rotis frozen stiff, sprinkled with rock salt and red chillies. I do not know what the calorie content was, but it was delicious under the circumstances. A brief rest and we headed down, with my companion asking questions incessantly: why are you punishing yourself and paying for it? Strange, you seem to be affluent; and so on and so forth. At some stage I lagged and he waited for me to catch up.

'You are having problems,' he tells me. And then, very nonchalantly, he gave me an offer.

'You were kind, so allow me to pay you back. Hop onto my back and I will carry you down to camp.'

I thought he was joking and said as much. But one look at his expression and I knew he was serious. He was too simple a man to be boasting. While the offer was made with all good intentions, I could not believe that he could carry me. And I was 65 kg, plus my pack with another 10 kg in it. Curiosity got the better of me and I said fine, let us give it a shot. For the next thirty minutes, he lugged me downhill with ease and would have continued if I had not stopped him.

It was such a minor act of kindness, sharing my meal, and he felt obliged to return the favour in the only way he could, as a poor porter. By offering to carry me back. For some strange reason, the gesture stayed with me forever. That simple act of sharing his limited sustenance on a brutal climb reminded me that gratitude is not about the riches we hold. It is about recognising the value in every small act of human kindness. This realisation echoes in the harsh realities of combat in my next anecdote.

Forgive me, but I did mention in the introduction that I am lazy. Allow me, therefore, to do a cut and paste of a short story I wrote years ago. The story was narrated to me by Major Sudhir Kumar Walia, SM (Bar), Ashok Chakra (posthumous), a day prior to his departure for the Kargil War. That was the last time anyone saw him south of the Banihal Pass. He was later killed in an anti-militant operation, somewhere on the heights of the Hafruda forest in Kupwara district. He was the most intrepid man I met, barring the militant Gul Mohammad (Pagal). But then, Gul's is a story I can never tell. Whenever I think of Sudhir, I am reminded of these lines from a poem by Kipling:

'A scrimmage in a border station—A canter down some dark defile—Two Thousand pounds of education—Drops to a ten-rupee jezail.'

Anyway, the story beckons.

The sun, a subdued orange ball, sank fast behind the Gagal ridge. In a matter of minutes, another day would end in the Kashmir Valley.

A black veil slowly covered the land. The mountain behind rose up to 3,000 metres and the Khobalmarghi top was now covered with a thick fog, rapidly rolling down the shoulders. Thunder rumbled across the valley and forked lightning lit up the Lolab Valley intermittently. Rain was imminent. The sound of insects and birds rose in unison to a crescendo. To those who knew the jungle, it was the last cry of the wild before silence descended with the night.

Major Sudhir Kumar looked up at the gloomy sky, then towards the village below. It had been one of those futile ambush operations where hours are spent waiting in the bushes. For men who had been out in the wilderness for the past 48 hours, the comforts of a house and a hot cup of tea were difficult to resist. The major looked back at his tired, hungry men and made up his mind.

'Balbir,' he said, calling the lead scout. 'Let us take a break in the village and wait for the vehicles.'

Selecting a big house at the periphery of the village, they made themselves comfortable. The major selected a corner next to the blazing hearth and stretched out his weary limbs, using his heavy pack as a pillow. The tension and fatigue of the past two days swept over him like a giant wave. An excited, loud chattering in Kashmiri from the next room disturbed him. He opened his eyes and told one of the men to see what was happening. A 10-year-old boy was ushered into the room. The boy was sobbing incessantly and his *firan* and boots were covered in mud.

'What is the matter, boy?' asked Sudhir. A woman behind him answered.

'*Jenab*, his father is sick. They have no money to treat him. He is trying to collect money from the villagers.'

'What is your name, boy?' asked the major.

'Amir,' he said, wiping the tears with the back of his sleeve.

'How much do you want?'

'A hundred rupees, for Abba's treatment in the clinic in Kupwara,' said Amir.

'And how do you plan to take him there?' asked Sudhir.

'I do not know. Nobody would like to move at this time of the night and if he does not get medical attention now, he will surely die by morning.'

Sudhir summoned the troop sergeant, instructing him to give

some cash to the boy. A few men were further detailed to carry the old man to the vehicle when it arrived.

'Amir,' he said, turning to the boy. 'I am going that way and we will give you a lift.'

They left Amir and his father at one of the local *hakims* (doctors) in town.

'Treat him well,' Sudhir told the doctor. 'I will come and check tomorrow. Don't worry,' he said, turning to Amir and tousling his grimy hair. 'He will be alright.'

'How should I return the money I have borrowed, *jenab*?' the boy asked in all seriousness.

'Forget it.' Sudhir said, smiling and then as an afterthought, he pulled the boy aside and added, 'If you ever get any information about militants, that's where I stay,' pointing at some dilapidated army barracks down the road. 'My name is Major Sudhir. You will remember that, won't you?'

Not long after meeting Amir, life settled back into a pattern familiar to soldiers in militant areas—eat, sleep, operations, with a constant hope of leave. Many months later, Sudhir was relaxing in his room when the sentry walked in.

'*Sahib*, there is a little boy at the gate. Says his name is Amir. Knows your name and is insisting on meeting you about something important.'

'Send him in,' said the major.

Sudhir sized up the little boy in a grey *firan* with a handsome face. The boy realised Sudhir had not recognised him. 'Sir…a few months ago, you gave me money to treat my father…'

'Oh, yes!' The major's face lit up. 'How is your father now?'

'Allah has spared him, *jenab*.'

'Have you come to return the money? I had told you to forget it,' said the major.

'No, *jenab*,' said Amir. 'You had asked me to come to you if I had any information on militants. I am here to give you that.'

The major pulled up a chair and told Amir to sit. 'Where, when and how many?' he asked in earnestness.

Amir paused, as if collecting his thoughts. His gaze fell on the crackling *bukhari* at his feet. Sudhir knew the boy was fighting his emotions. He needed help in parting with the information.

'You need not worry. Amir,' Sudhir said. 'No one will know you gave the information. And if you are feeling guilty, forget it. You are ridding the country of vermin. Maybe when you grow up, we can get you a job in the army.'

The boy took a deep breath and answered slowly. 'One man is at my house. If you can come quietly and before dark, you may get him.'

Sudhir did not press the boy for more information. He had shown enough courage for his age, coming all the way from his village to an army post. The major stood up and crossed the room to a map hanging on the wall. He ran his eyes over it more out of habit than for information, for he knew the area like the back of his hand. Soon, orders were being passed down to the men's quarters and a fighting patrol was ready within minutes. Sudhir addressed the men.

'From here to the *ziyarat* in vehicles. I will get off with 10 men, the rest continue to Charkoot. Stay on the radio in case I need reserves. My party will skirt the village till we reach the house. Remember, speed and surprise are essential. Any doubts or questions?'

There were none. Each man knew his role. They approached the village and the major watched, like a worried father, as his men broke out in the field outside and stealthily closed in towards the target house. This was the crucial stage where surprise could be lost. A while later, Sudhir surveyed his men in position around the house and a satisfied smile played on his lips. They were good, he thought. They were his boys after all.

The house was insignificant compared to the neighbour's and in crying need of repairs. The house, in a way, reflected the family's affluence or the lack of it and it made sense as to why they did not have a hundred rupees to treat the father. He imagined the militant sitting around, ordering and bullying the family members for food and money. The thought angered him. A local was summoned and sent into the house with a message for the militant to surrender. The answer came back as negative. A brief pause, as the residents of the house exited and then the firefight started.

The odds were stacked heavily against the man holed up inside. A grenade through the window brought the curtains down on the engagement. His death got him *jannat* (heaven), it got Major Sudhir Kumar and his troop another kill, and as Sudhir thought, it was one less to fight for Jehad-e-Kashmir. As the militant's blood-soaked body was pulled out of the house, a soulful, keening wail rose up from the villagers around. Sudhir had heard it before and it always sent a shiver up his spine. He knew immediately that the dead man was a local. As a mark of respect, he saluted the corpse. The words from a poem he knew came to him. 'No sight better below the blue sky than to see how bravely a man can die.'

The major turned and gave one last look at the house and the surroundings, memorising the details of the incident for a debrief later. Gradually, the onlookers drifted back to their houses. Under the shadows of a walnut tree, Sudhir saw Amir. He stood next to an old man, holding his hand. Glancing around to ensure that nobody was watching, Sudhir strolled up to them.

'Your father, Amir, I presume,' said the major. 'Looks fine now. Well done boy, that was man's work and it takes courage to do what you did.' Taking a couple of hundred-rupee notes from his pocket, he crumpled them into a ball and extended his hand towards Amir, saying,

'*Inaam* (reward), for what you did and if you drop in at the post tomorrow, I will buy you a tape recorder from the canteen.'

'*Shukriya,*' said Amir in a quivering voice, 'I did not do it for the money.' That is when Sudhir noticed that both the father and the son were silently crying.

'You saved my father's life,' continued Amir. 'In return, I gave you something which you hold precious as a soldier, the life of another man. You owe me nothing. For what price in the world, *huzoor,* can you pay me for killing my only brother? Remember us in your prayers. *Khuda hafiz.*'

The old man and the boy turned around and still holding hands in their grief, walked back up the hill. With a lump in his throat, Sudhir watched them go until they disappeared into the darkness.

As I mentioned at the beginning of this chapter, there is a reason I felt compelled to speak about gratitude.

As a combat soldier, I have had my share of close shaves—moments where luck, instinct and something far greater conspired to pull me back and preserve me. I walked out of some tight situations with my life intact and barring a nagging lower back injury from a night jump, without any major physical damage. A cheap price, really, for all the risks we took.

Many were not so lucky. Not everyone came back whole. And I am not just talking about the fallen in battle. Some left the service with knees that would never heal, spines forever damaged, bodies broken not in combat—but in training.

In that contrast—between what could have been and what was—I learned the value of gratitude. It grounds you. It humbles you. It reminds you that you are not invincible, but you are blessed.

Whether it was on a wind-blasted ridge at 14,000 feet, or in an insurgency-ridden village where a stranger offered me tea and a quiet place to sit, I was reminded again and again that life is a mosaic of small mercies—and that we must learn to see them, acknowledge them and give thanks for them.

In your own journey—whether you are walking through chaos or quiet comfort—never forget to pause and take stock of what you do have. The breath in your lungs. The people who love you. The people who helped and showed kindness. The second chance you did not think you would get.

Gratitude is not weakness. It is a virtue that clears the fog, centres your mind and reminds you that life is worth fighting for.

Takeaways

- ***Be conscious of the fleeting nature of time.*** *It slips through our hands faster than we realise and once gone, it never returns. Value it. Guard it. Use it well.*
- ***Take a moment to step back from the noise and look at your life—not through the lens of what is missing, but with an appreciation for what is.*** *Breath in your lungs.*

People who care. A body that still moves. A mind that still questions.

- ***Be thankful—not just in grand gestures, but in the quiet acknowledgments****. The kind word. The second chance. The favour done without fanfare.*
- ***Gratitude is not about grandiosity—it is about presence.*** *It is about recognising that even amidst the chaos, you are still here. And that, in itself, is something to be grateful for.*
- ***Let that thankfulness be your anchor****. Let it be your strength. And let it remind you, always, to live with a little more awareness, a little more humility and a lot more heart.*

ACKNOWLEDGEMENT

To an existential vacuum and boredom.

BIBLIOGRAPHY

Books

Christopher McDougall, *Natural Born Heroes: How a Daring Band of Misfits Mastered the Lost Secrets of Strength and Endurance*, Knopf, 2015.

Colin Powell, *It Worked For Me: In Life and Leadership*, Harper, 2014.

Darren Moore, *The Soldier: A History of Courage, Sacrifice and Brotherhood*, Icon Books, 2009.

Lord Moran, *The Anatomy of Courage*, Constable, 1945.

Rupal Patel, *From CIA to CEO: Unconventional Life Lessons for Thinking Bigger, Leading Better and Being Bolder*, Bonnier Books, 2022.

Seneca, *Letters from a Stoic*, Penguin Classics, 2014.

Articles

S. Lyubomirsky, K.M. Sheldon and D. Schkade, 'Pursuing happiness: The architecture of sustainable change'. *Review of General Psychology*, 2005. 9(2), pp.111–131. https://doi.org/10.1037/1089-2680.9.2.111

Amazon Customer Reviews

★★★★½ 4.5 out of 5 stars

There is a vacuum in the field of war fiction in India and Abhay's book fills it.—*The Hindu*

The book engrosses you and transports you to the beautiful Lolab Valley in Kashmir ripped apart time and again by violence and bloodshed.
—*Mumbai Mirror*

The nerve tingling tale of battles between soldiers and terrorists is interspersed with the narrative of love in all its complex shades. —*The Tribune*

In the Valley of Shadows
ISBN: 978-81-8328-184-3 • ₹395

Amazon Customer Reviews

★★★★½ 4.6 out of 5 stars

An action-packed and fast-paced read.—*Business Standard*

Abhay Sapru offers a unique perspective of the Sri Lankan War in an engaging, page-turning account of the clash between the Indian Peace Keeping Force and the LTTE, with voices from both sides of what will go down as one of history's great tragedies.
—*Shashi Tharoor*

The Beckoning Isle
ISBN: 978-81-8328-491-2 • ₹395

Amazon Customer Reviews

★★★★½ 4.6 out of 5 stars

A fascinating story written in superb language! It will not allow you to put down the book till it is finished. Having operated in counter-militancy operations along the Shamshabari Range and on either side of Pir Panjal Range in Jammu & Kashmir, I find the description of the terrain, locales and combat activities as authentic as can be. Only a Special Forces officer can go into such details.

—**Gen VP Malik** (Retd),
Former Chief of Army Staff

The Savage Hills
ISBN 978-81-8328-549-0 • ₹ 395